HOW TO DRAW CUTE PETS & ANIMALS

A FUN AND SIMPLE STEP BY STEP ANIME DRAWING BOOKS FOR BEGINNERS. LEARN EASY TO DRAW KAWAII FOR ARTISTS, CARTOONISTS, AND DOODLERS

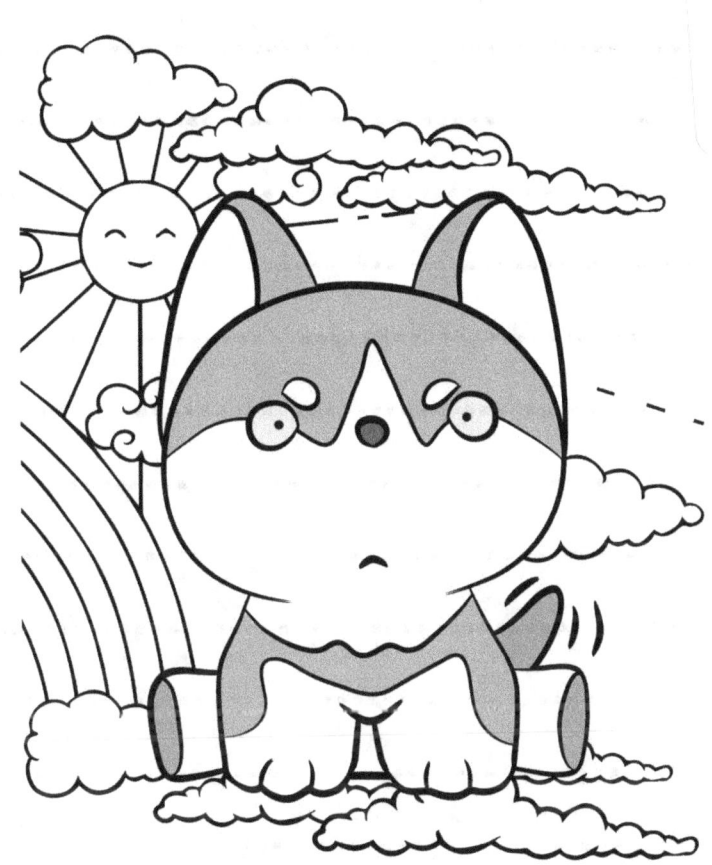

BOOK AND COVER DESIGN BY PHOO PUNYA

ISBN: 9781070916798

FIRST EDITION: MAY 2019

TABLE OF CONTENT

HOW TO DRAW

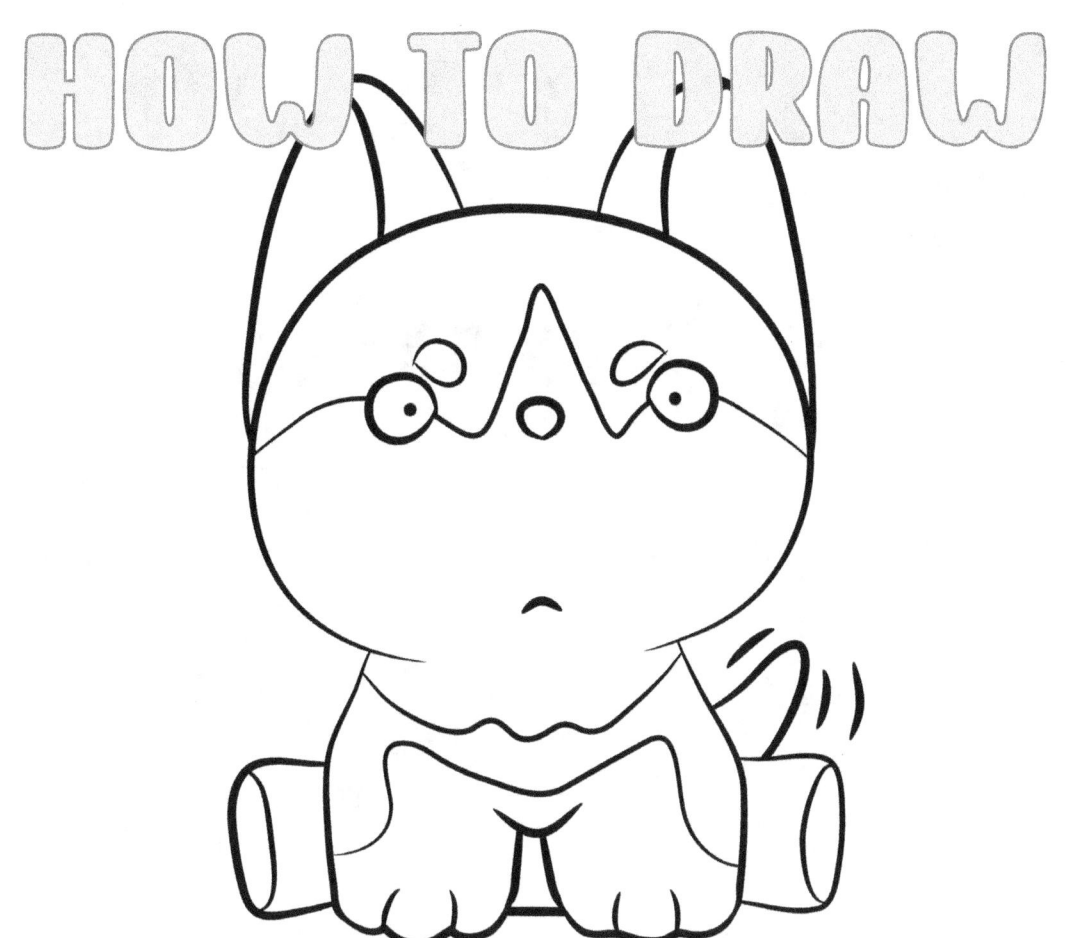

CUTE PETS

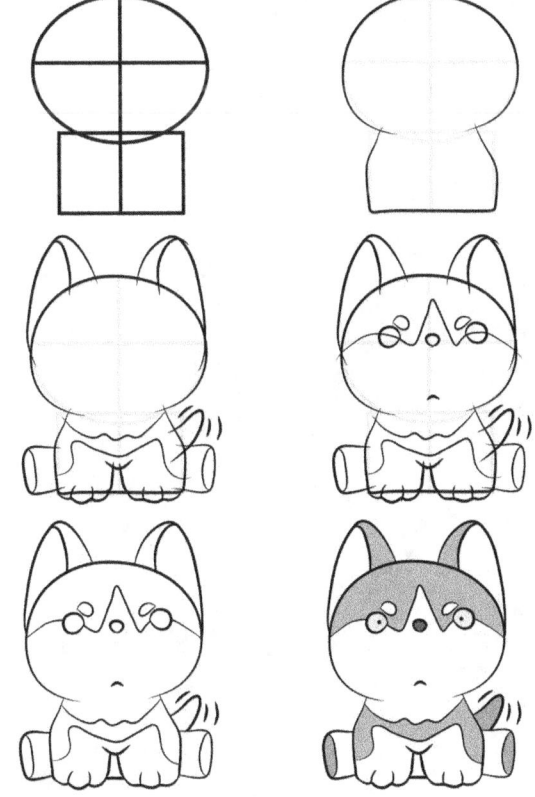

ANIMALS

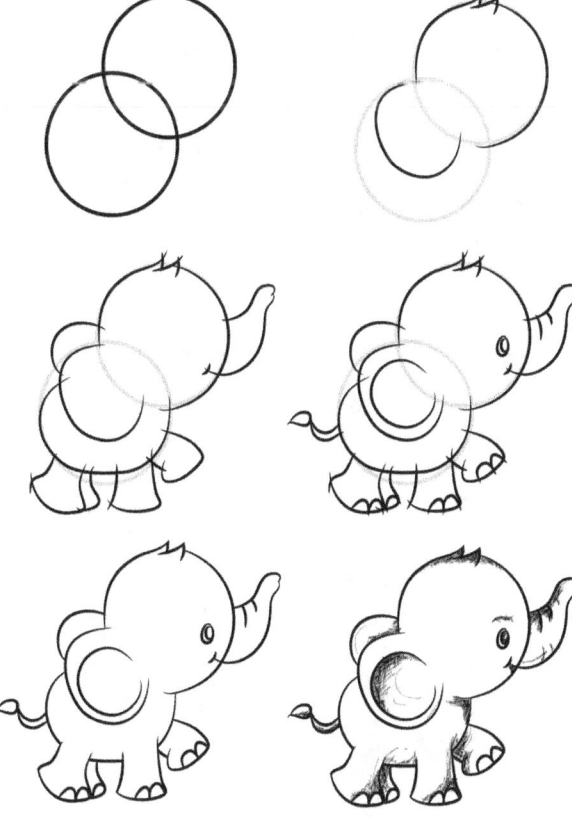

DOG

JUMP

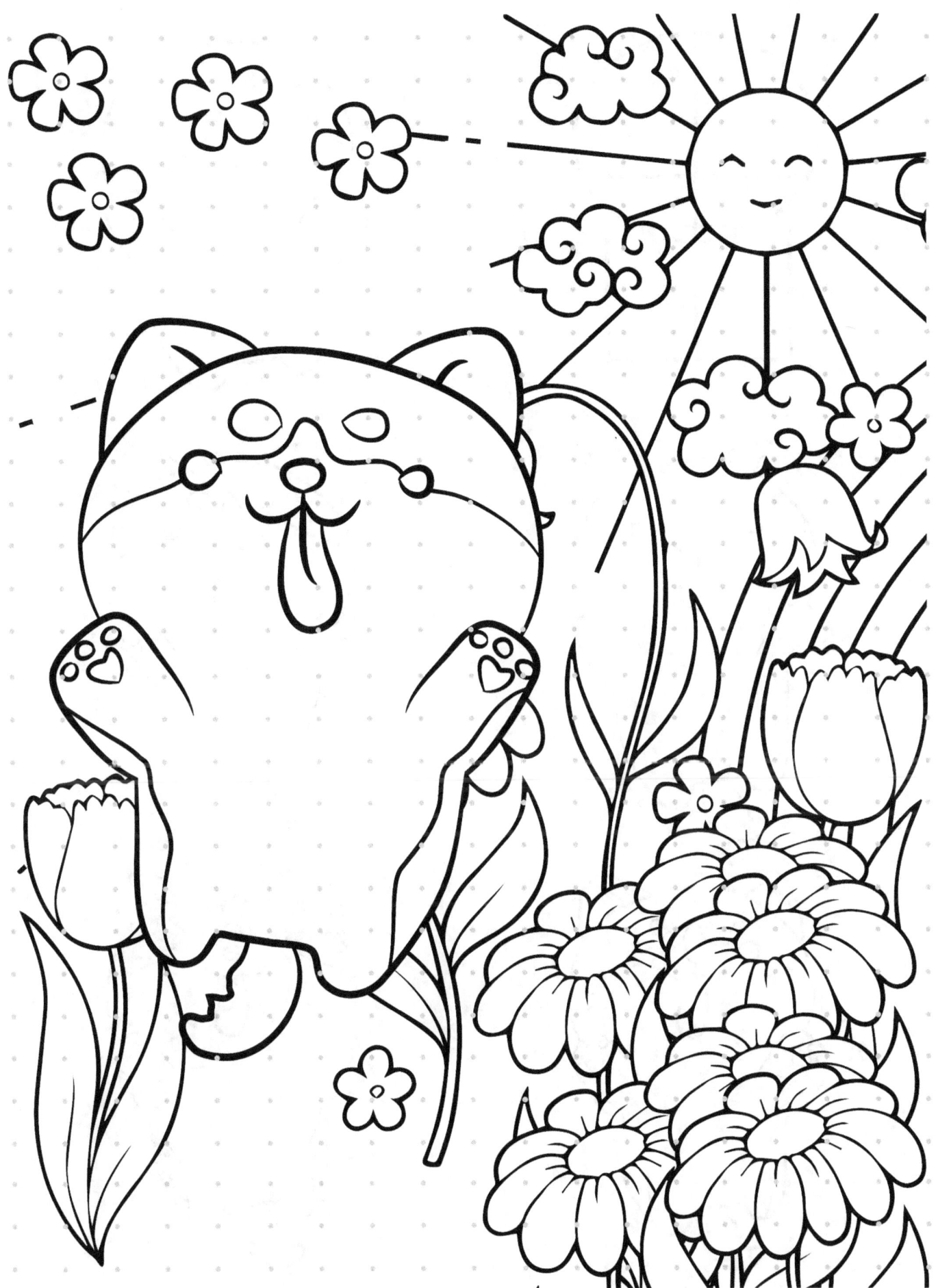

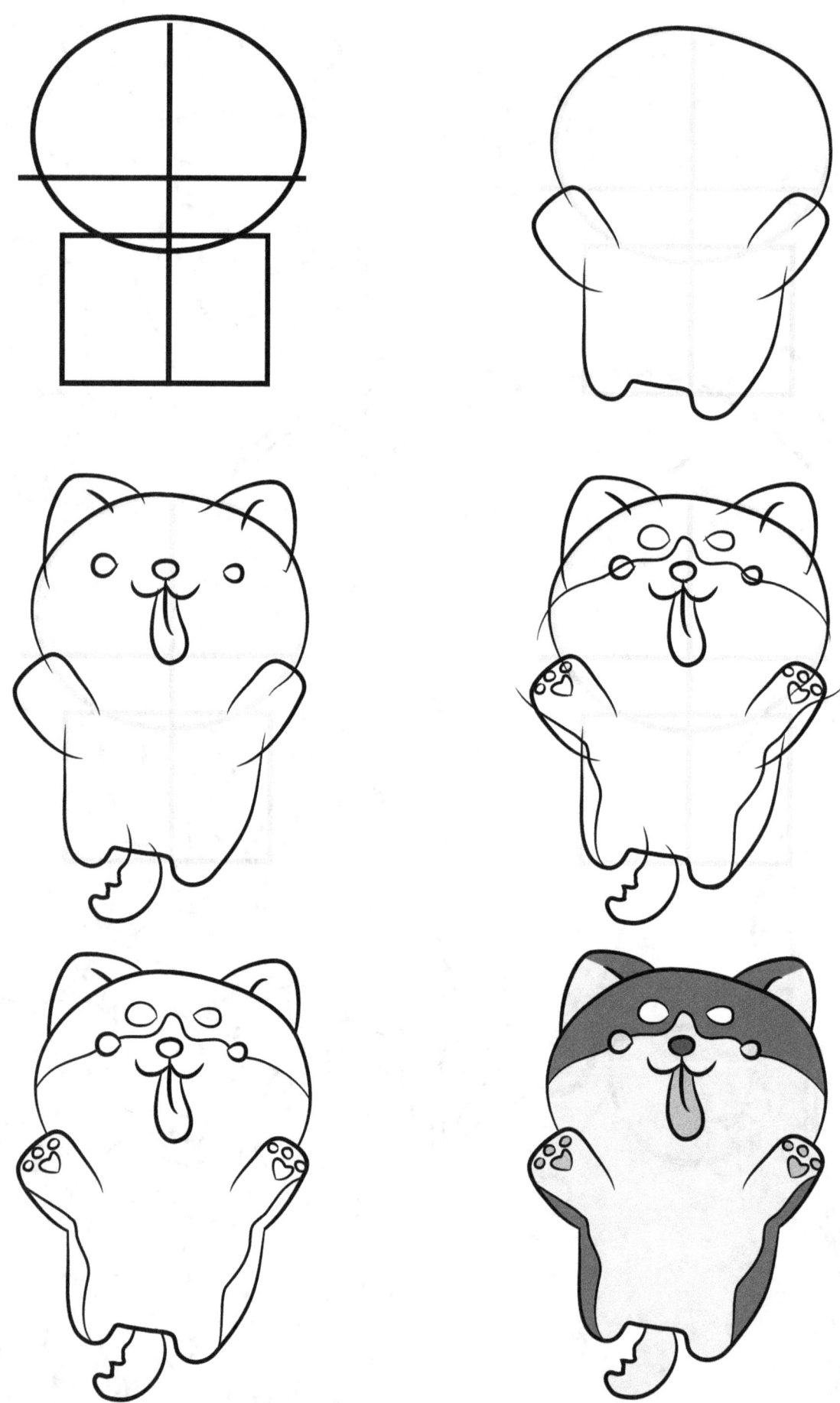

DOG SIT

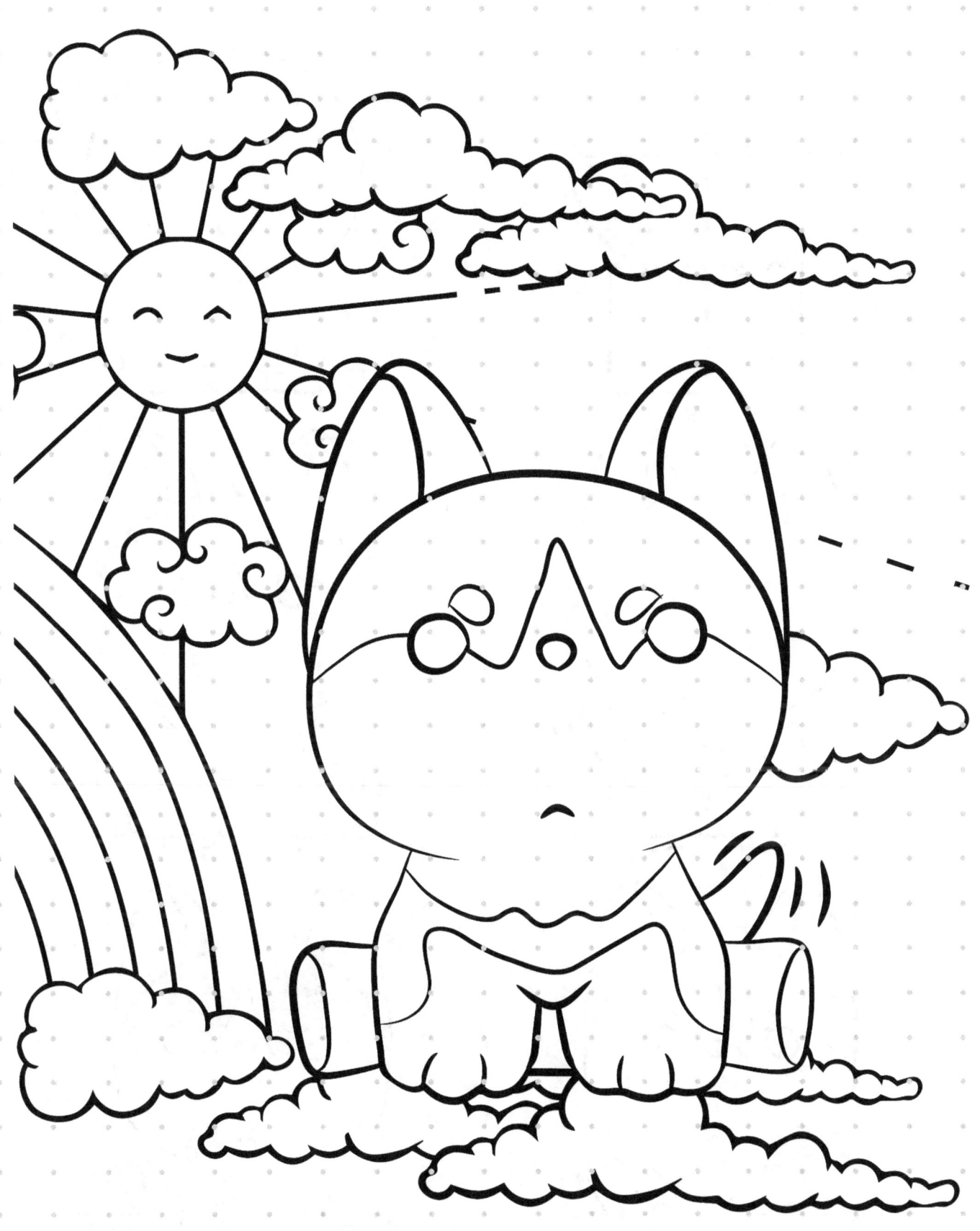

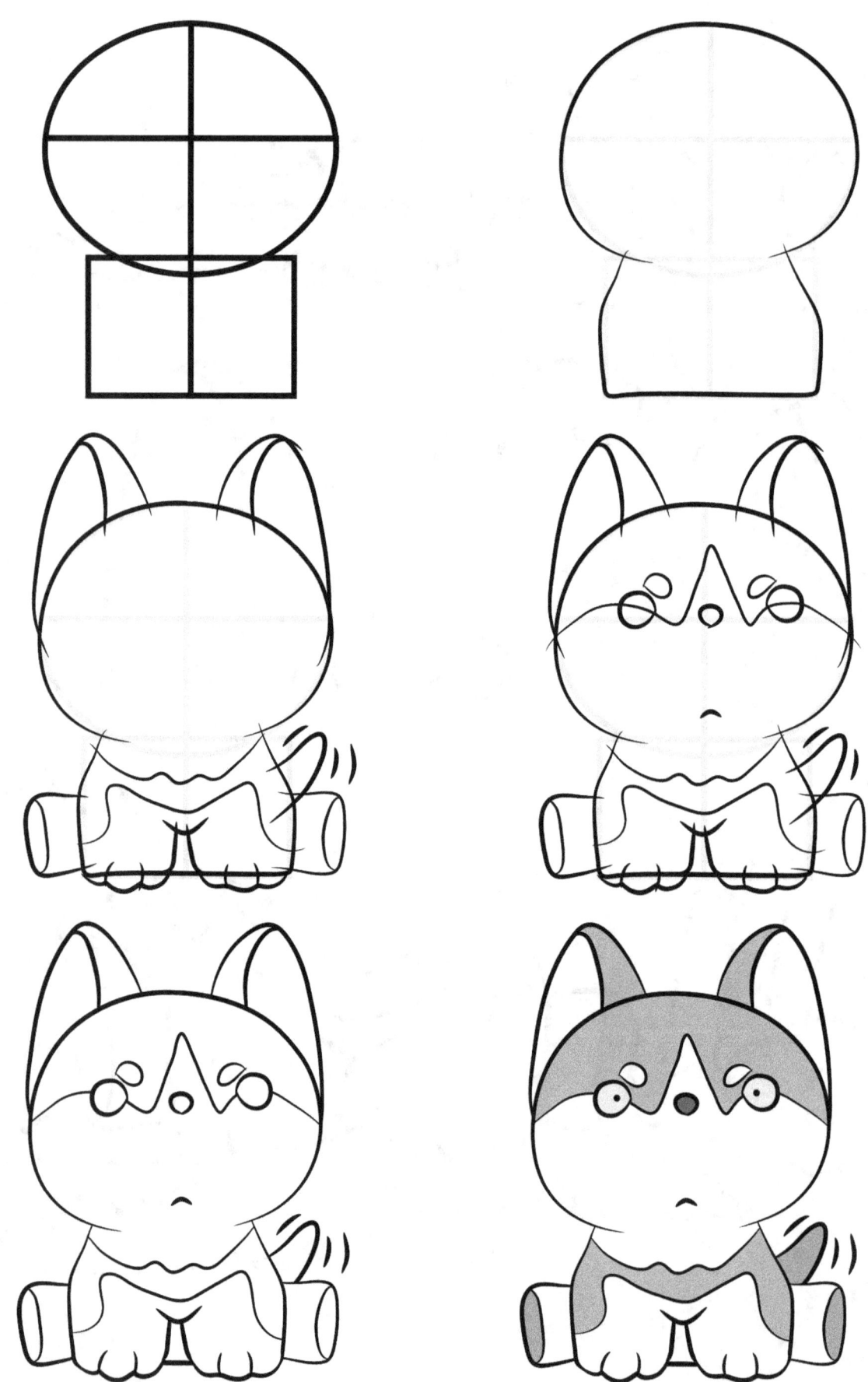

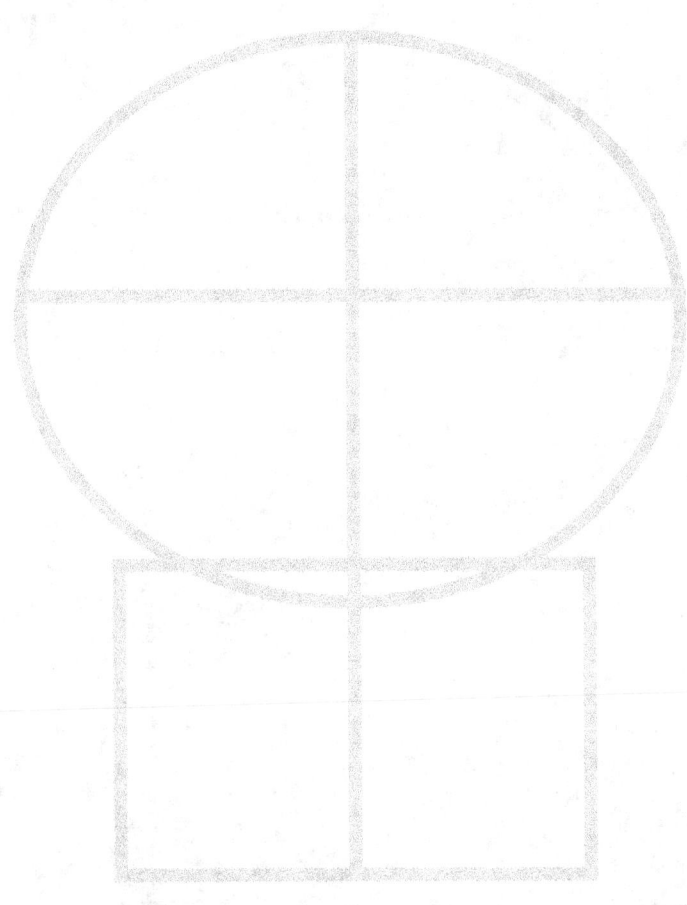

CAT
WALK

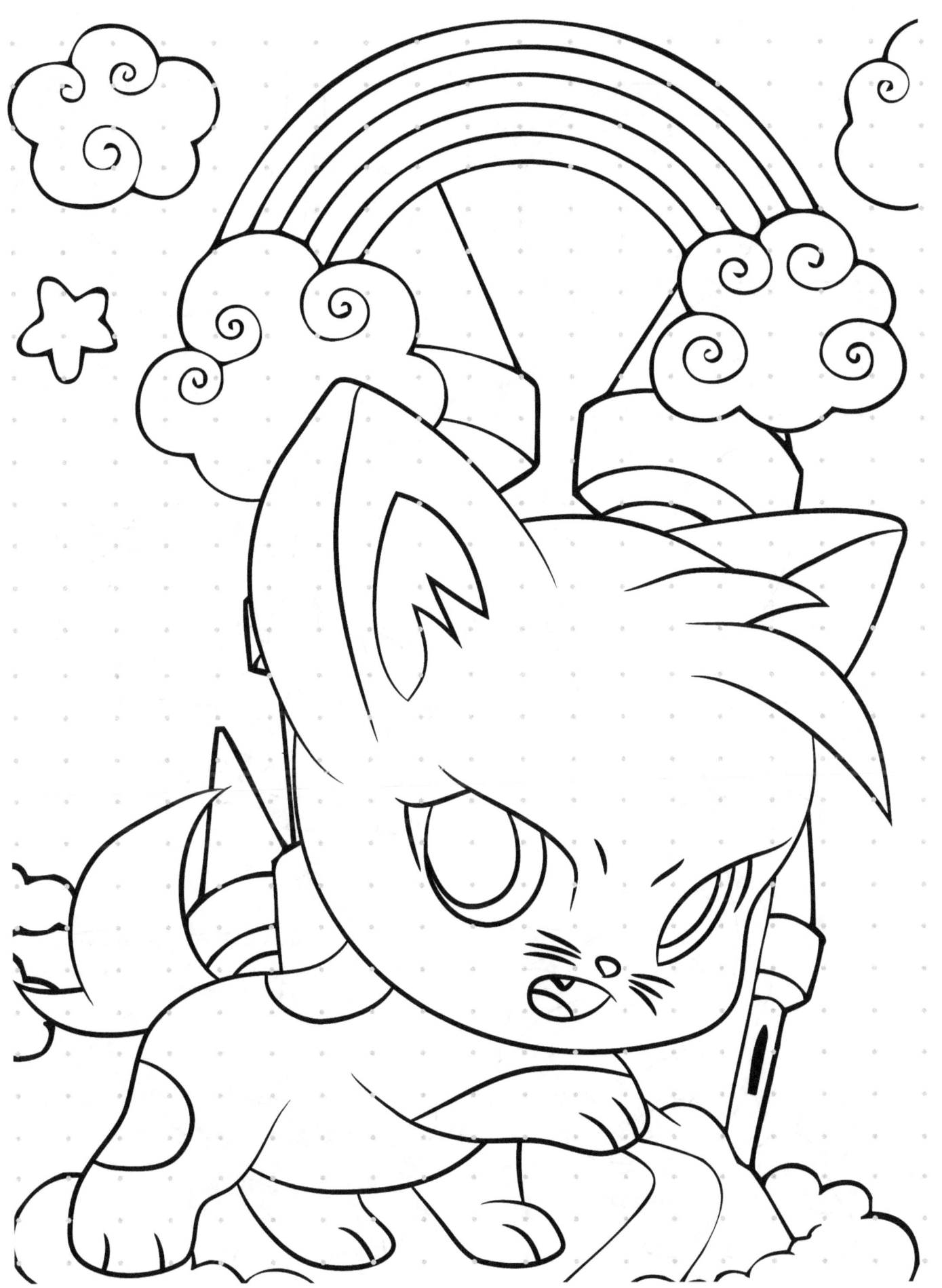

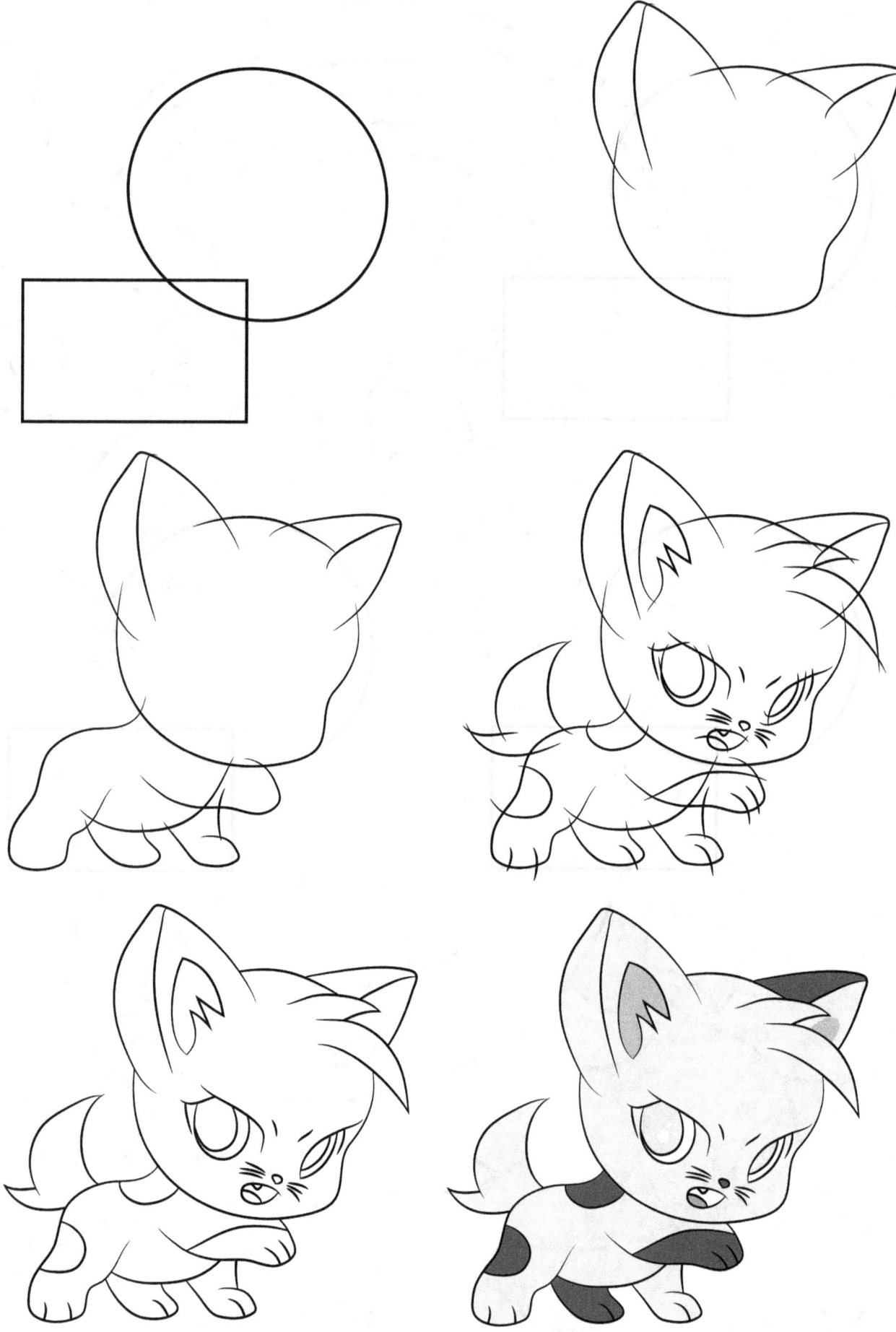

CAT
SIT

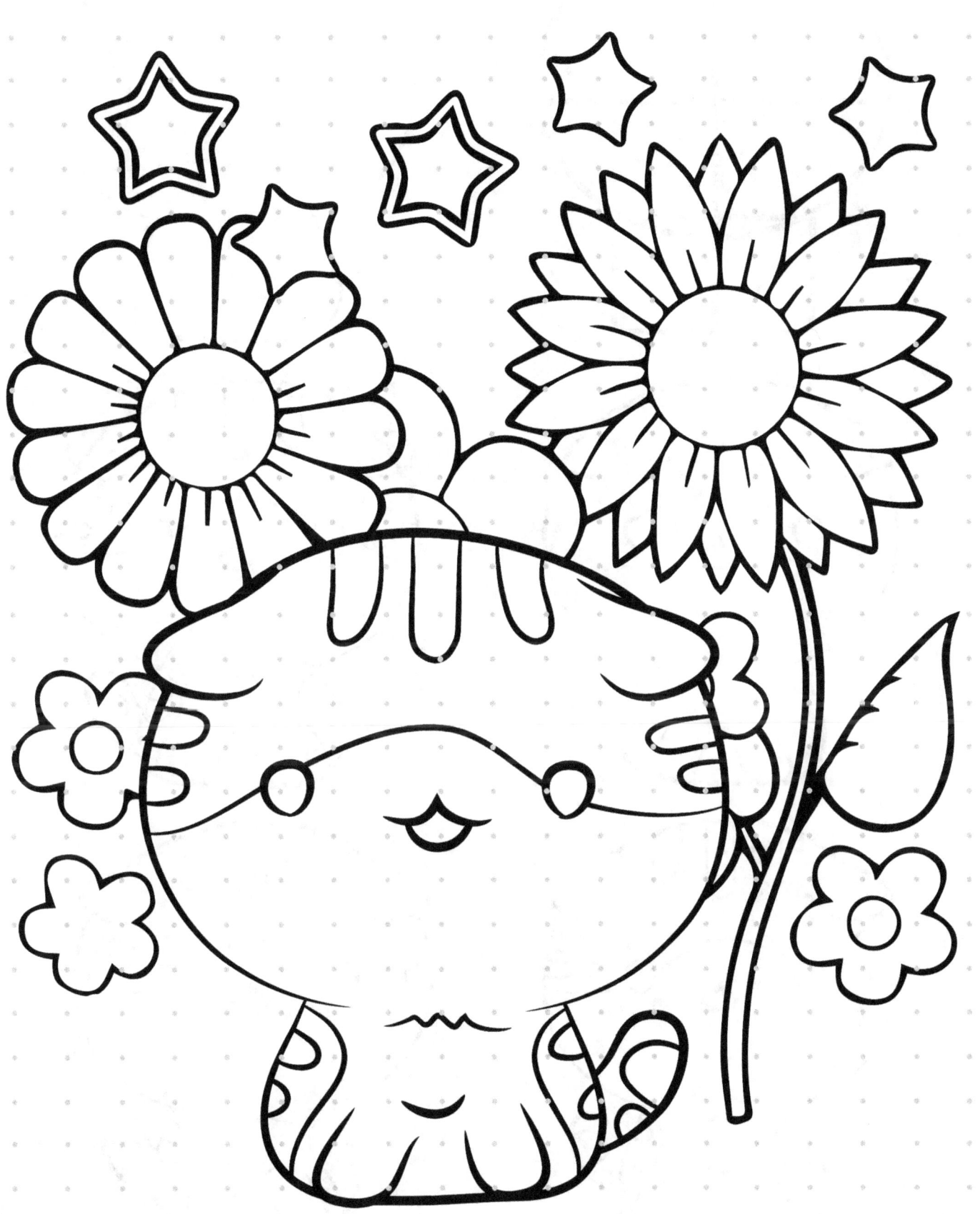

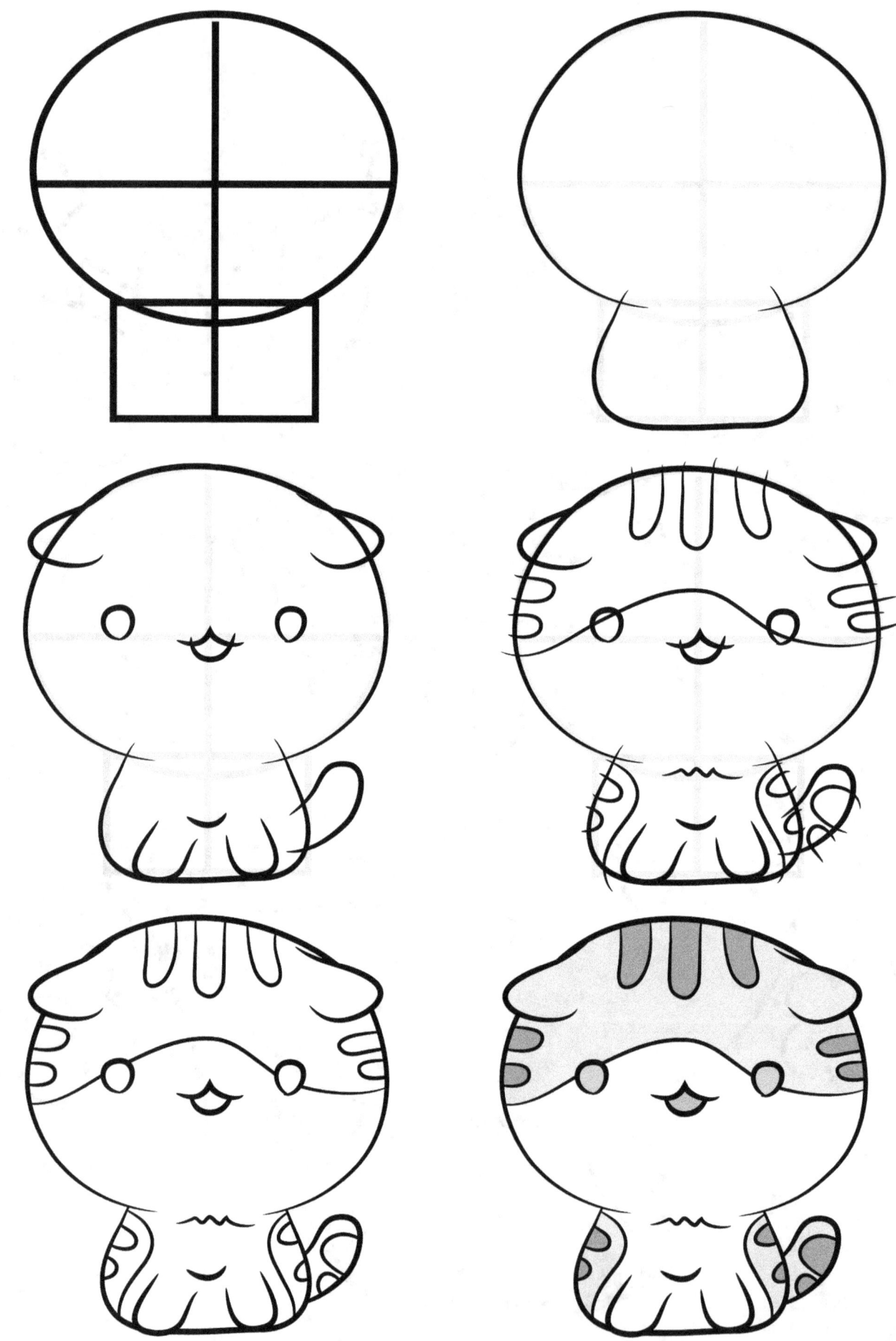

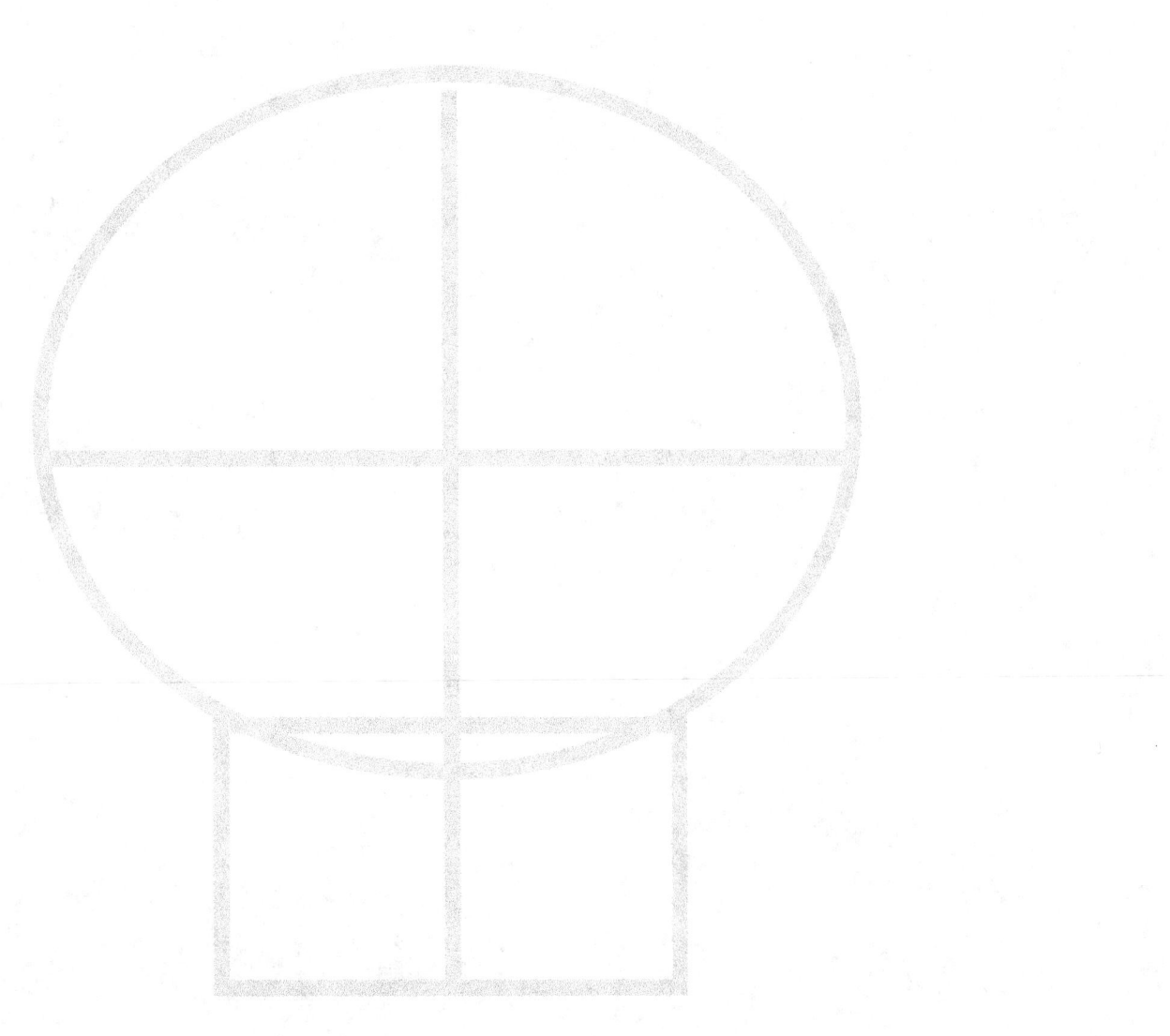

CAT
SIT

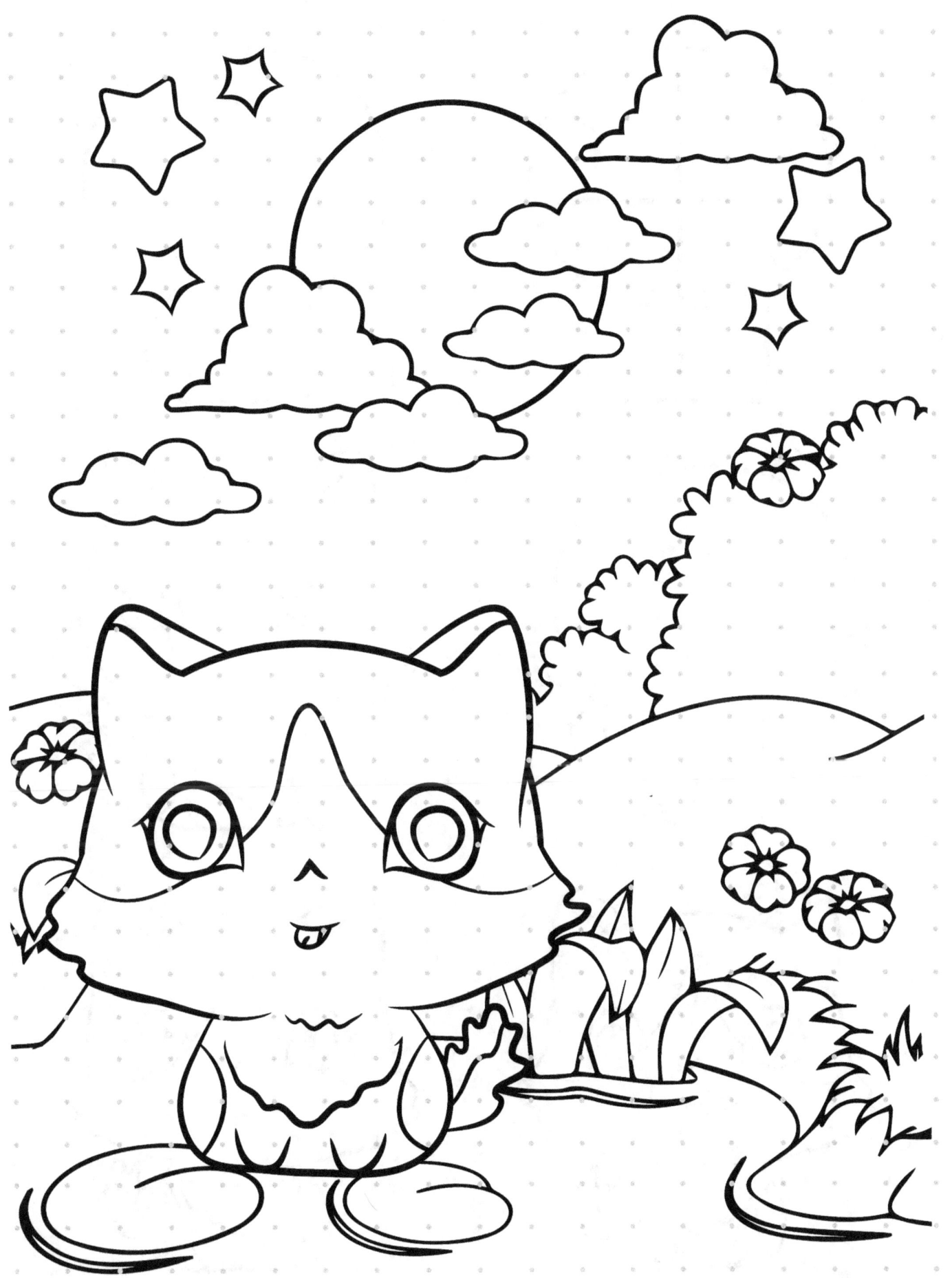

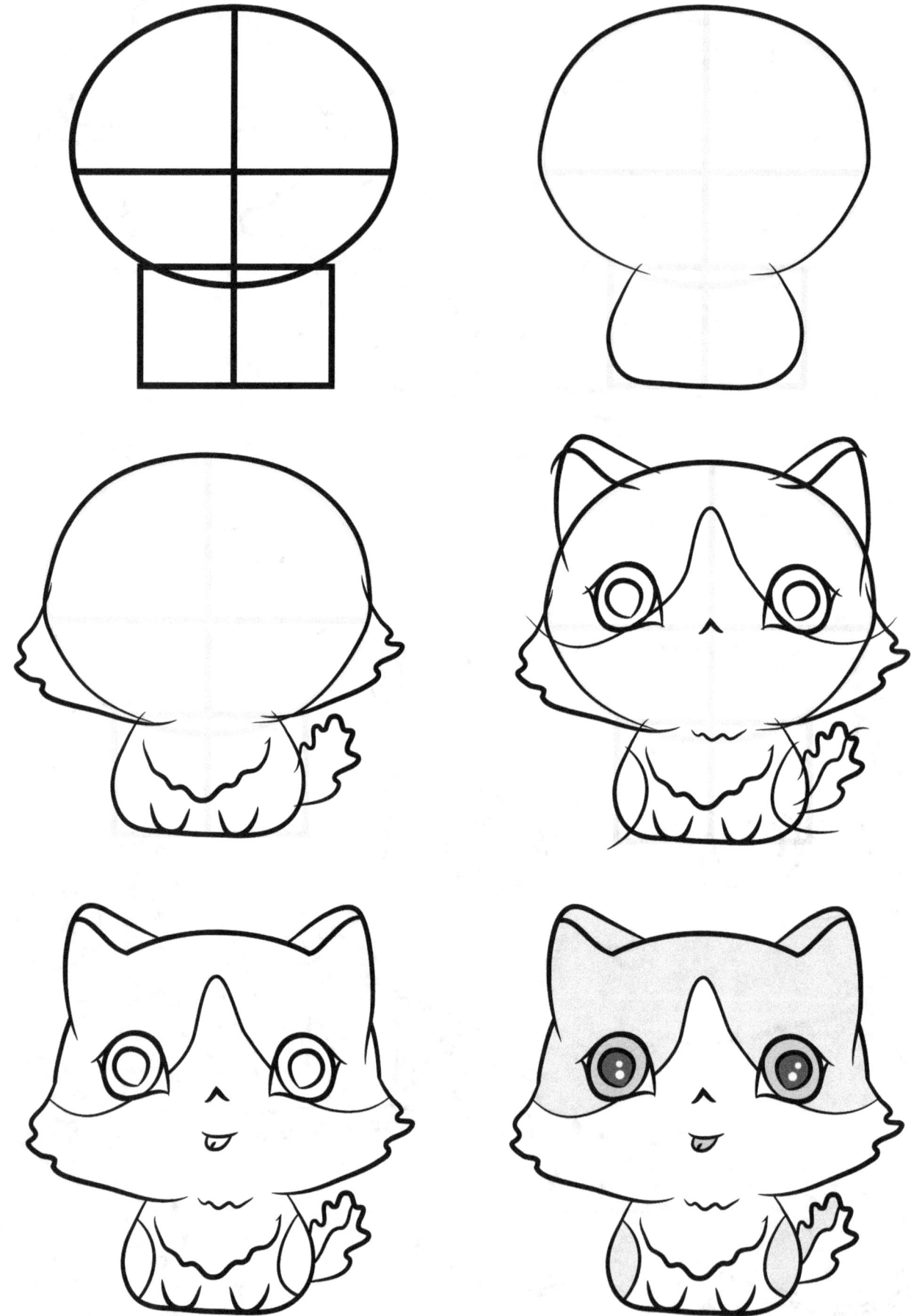

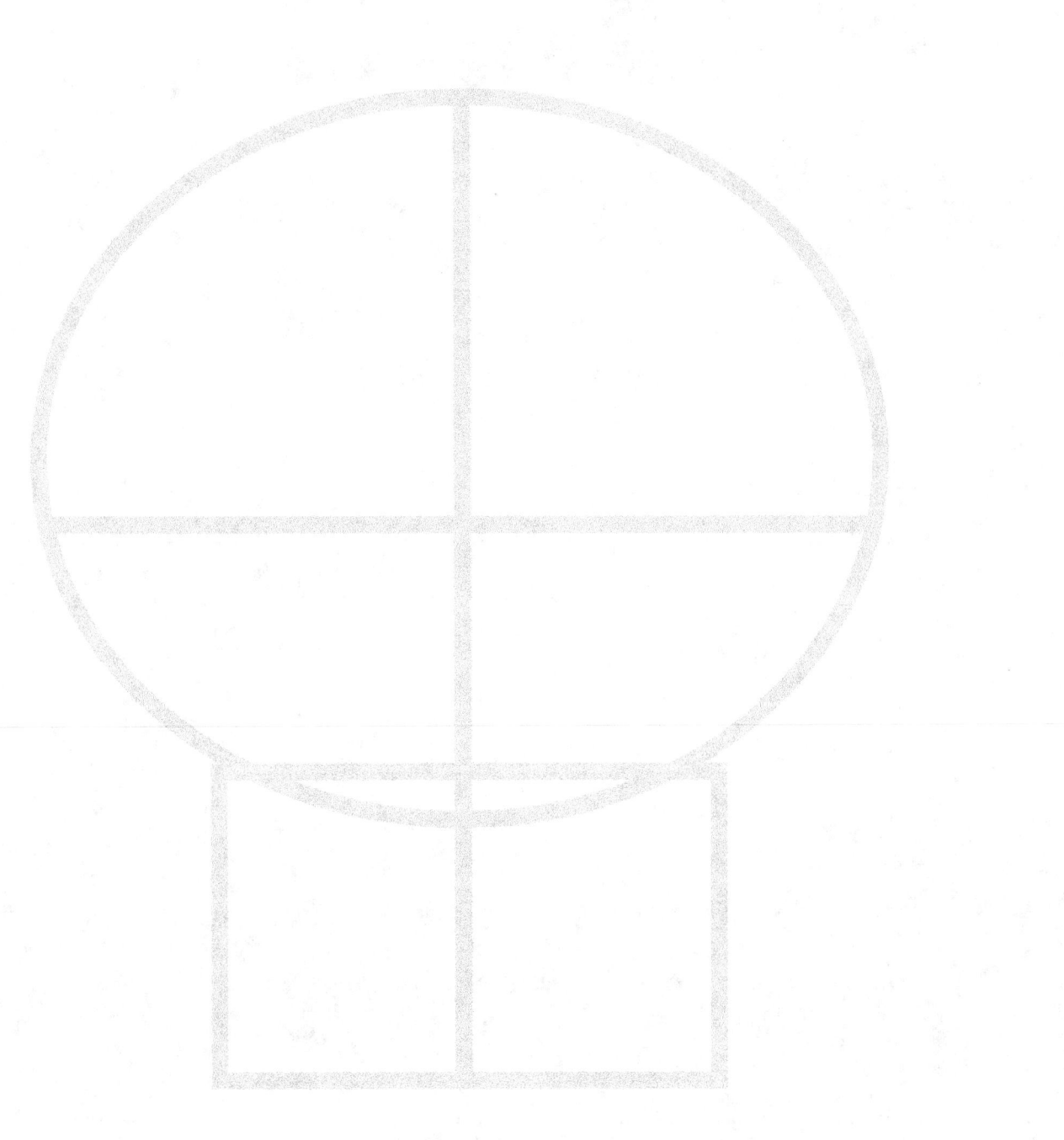

WOLF
STAND

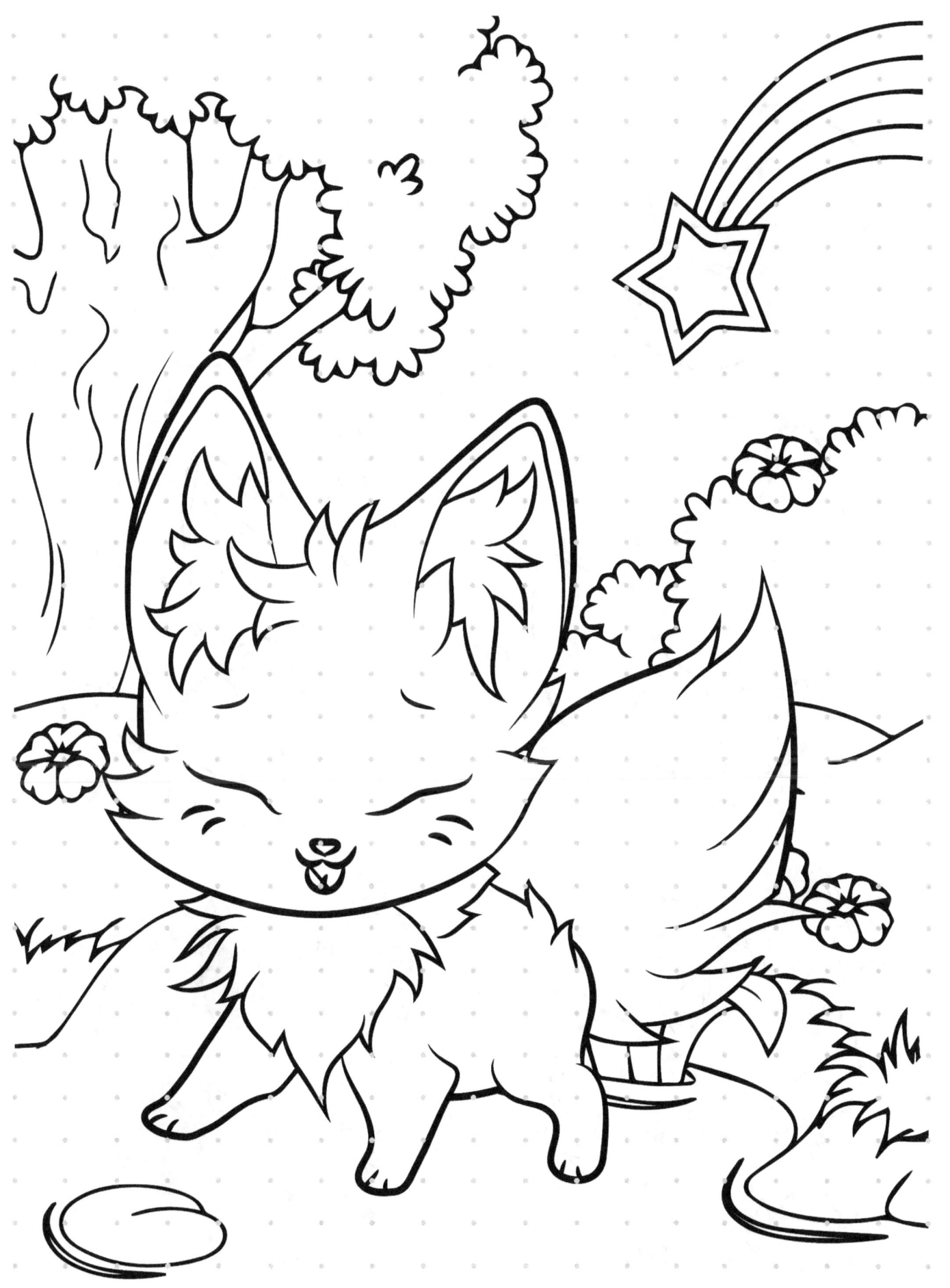

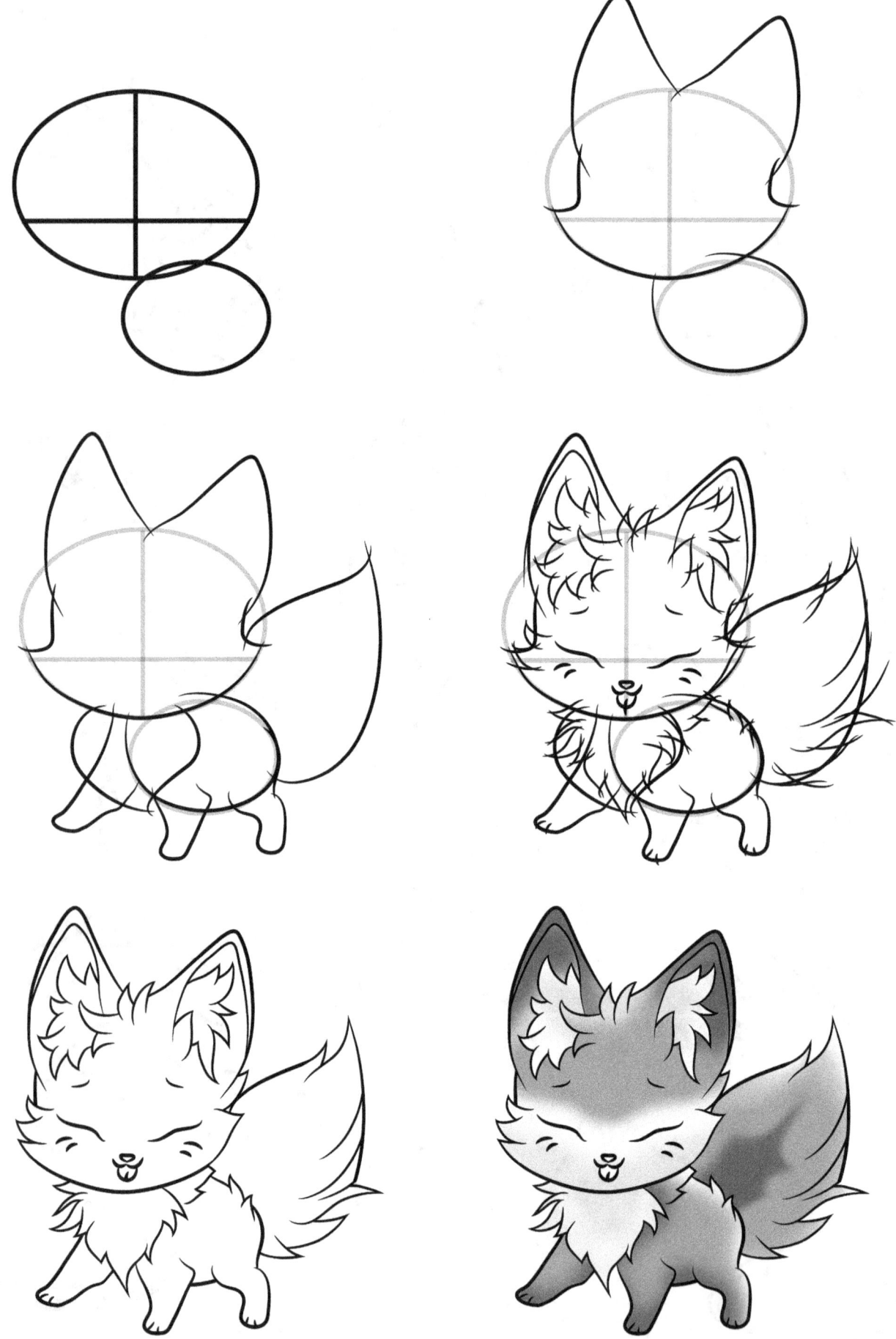

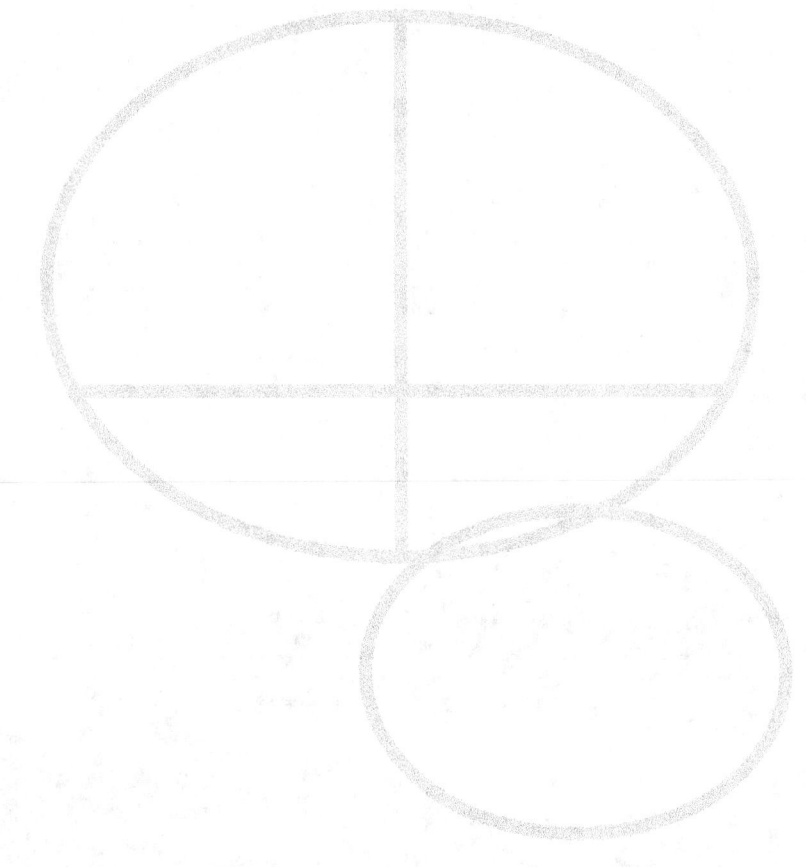

WOLF
SIT

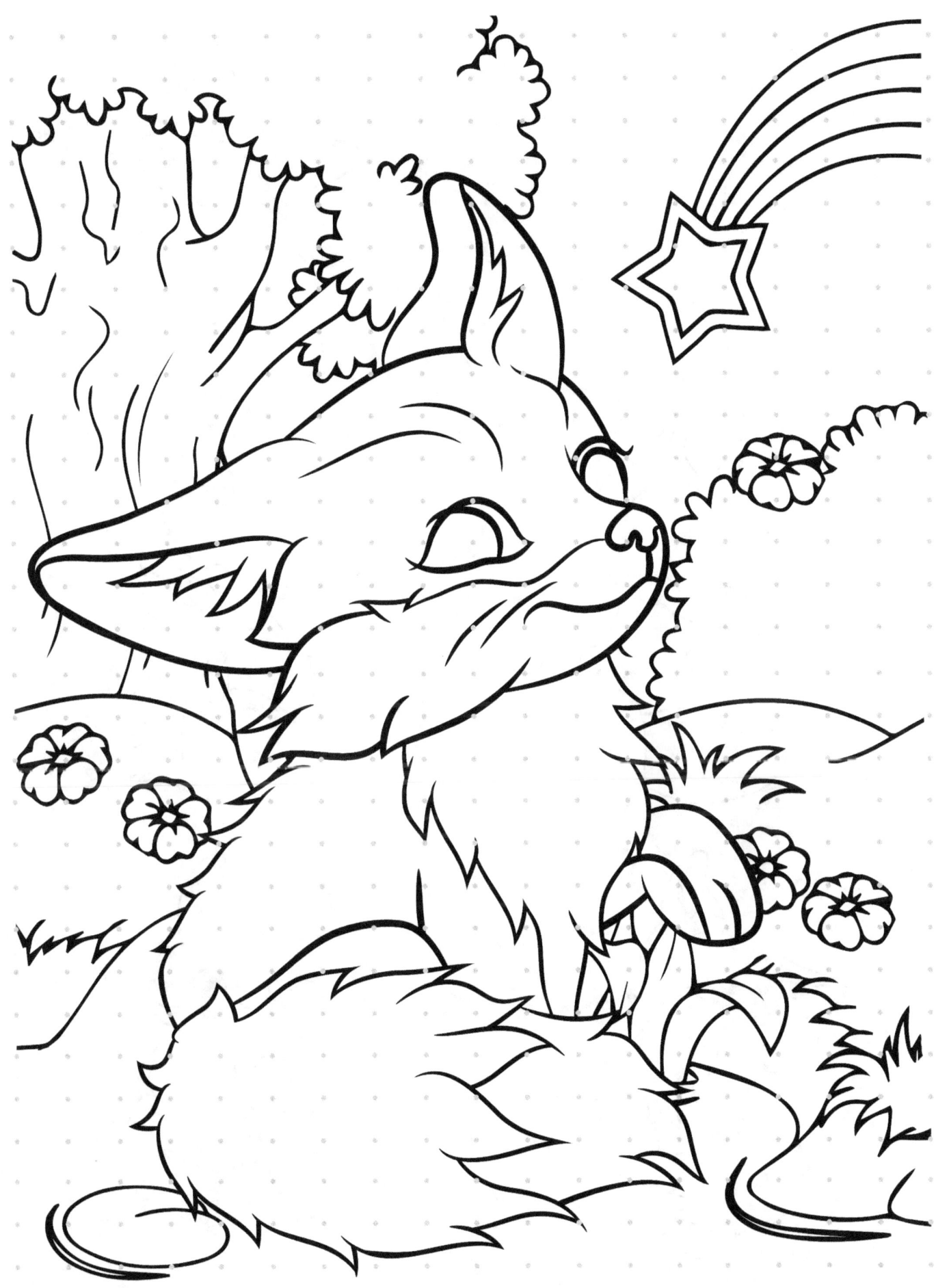

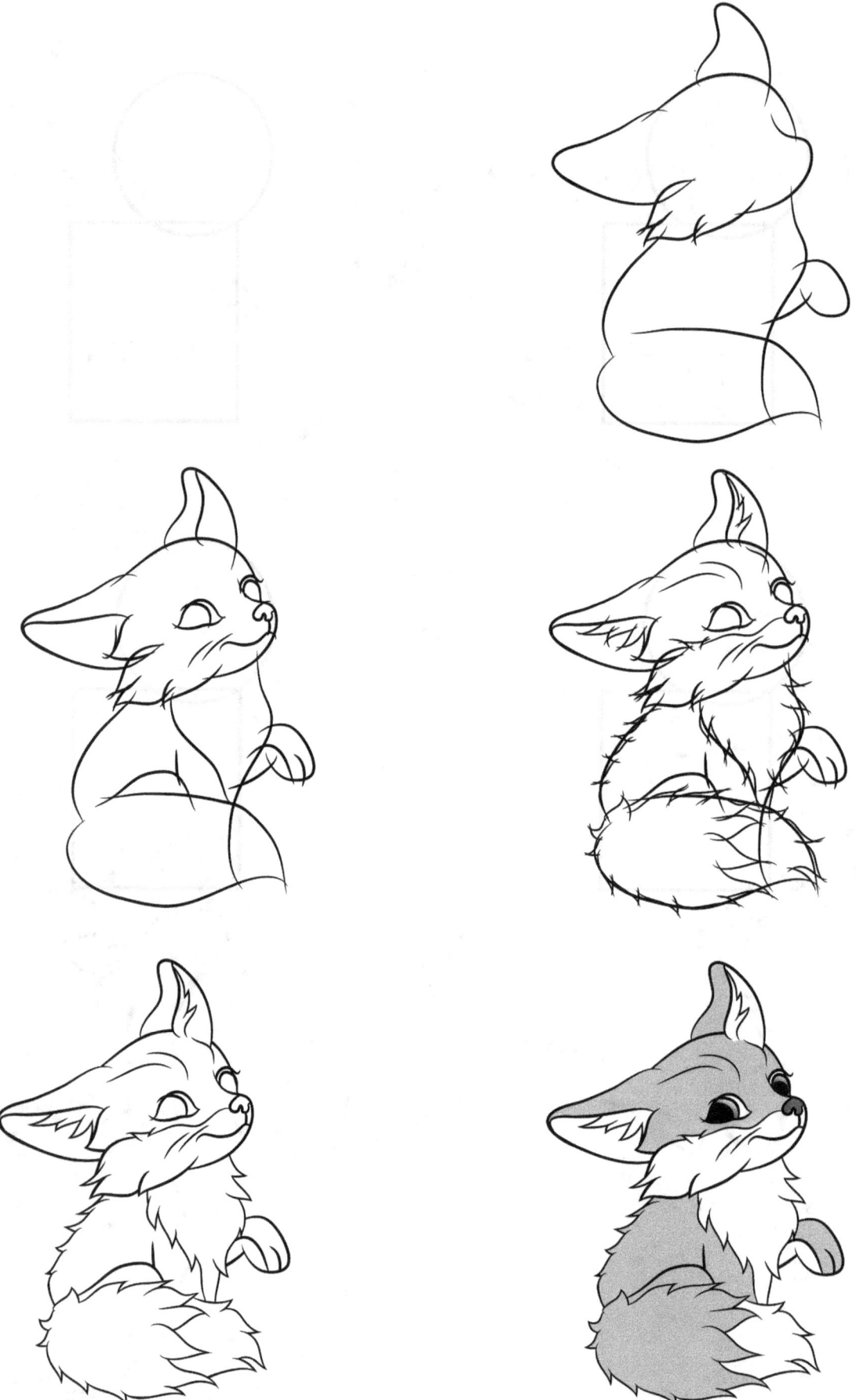

SQUIRREL STAND

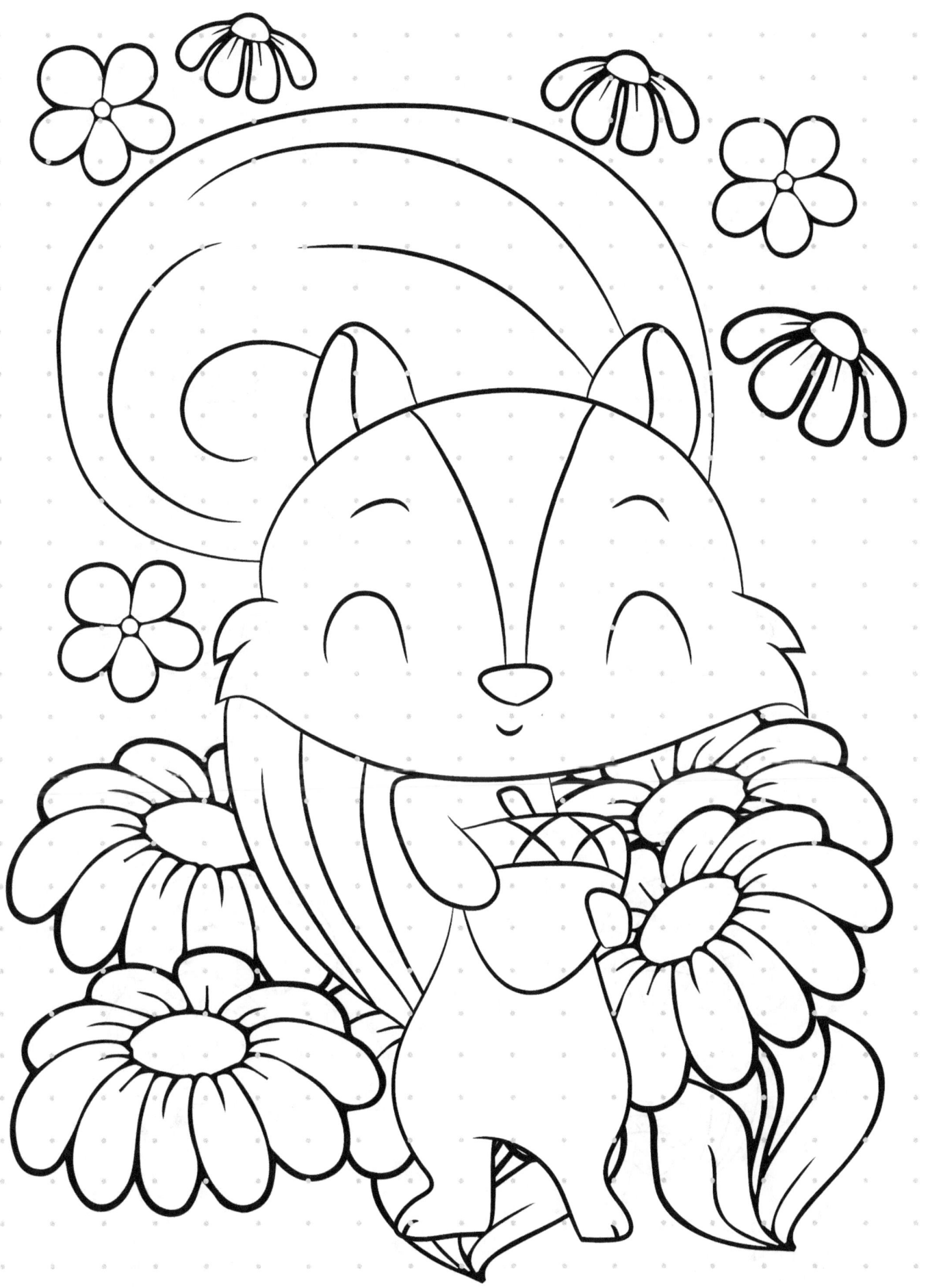

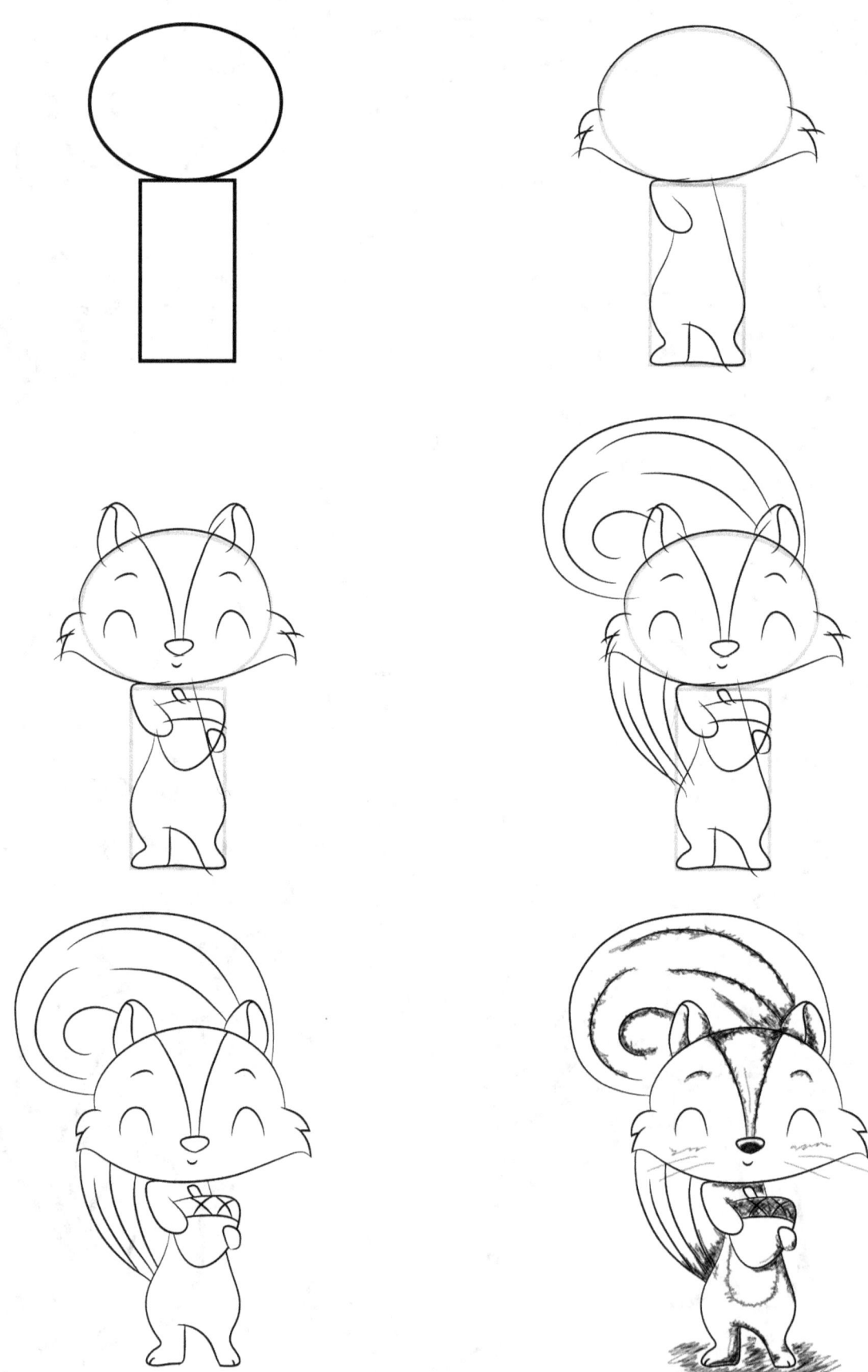

RABBIT
PLAY

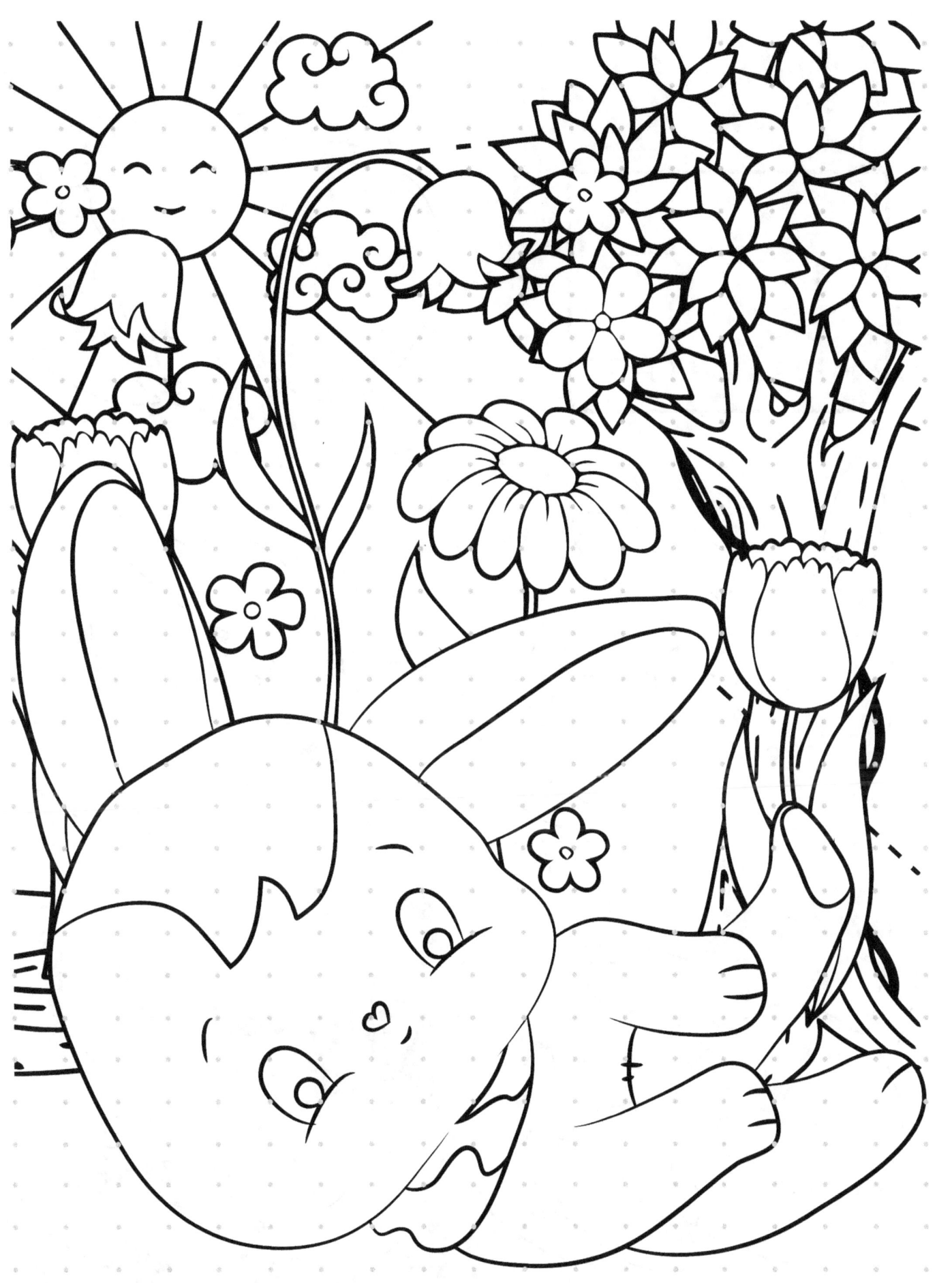

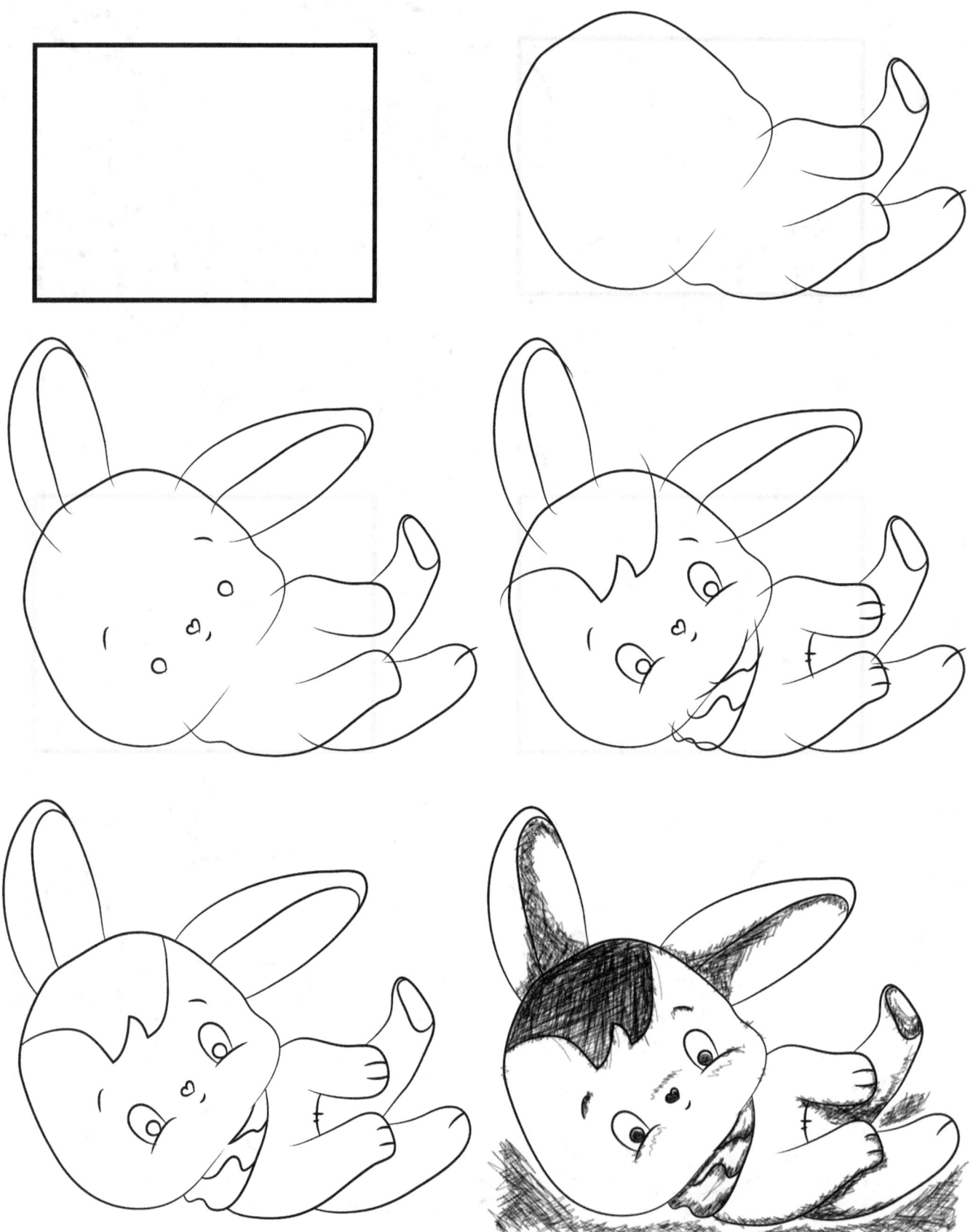

COW
SIT

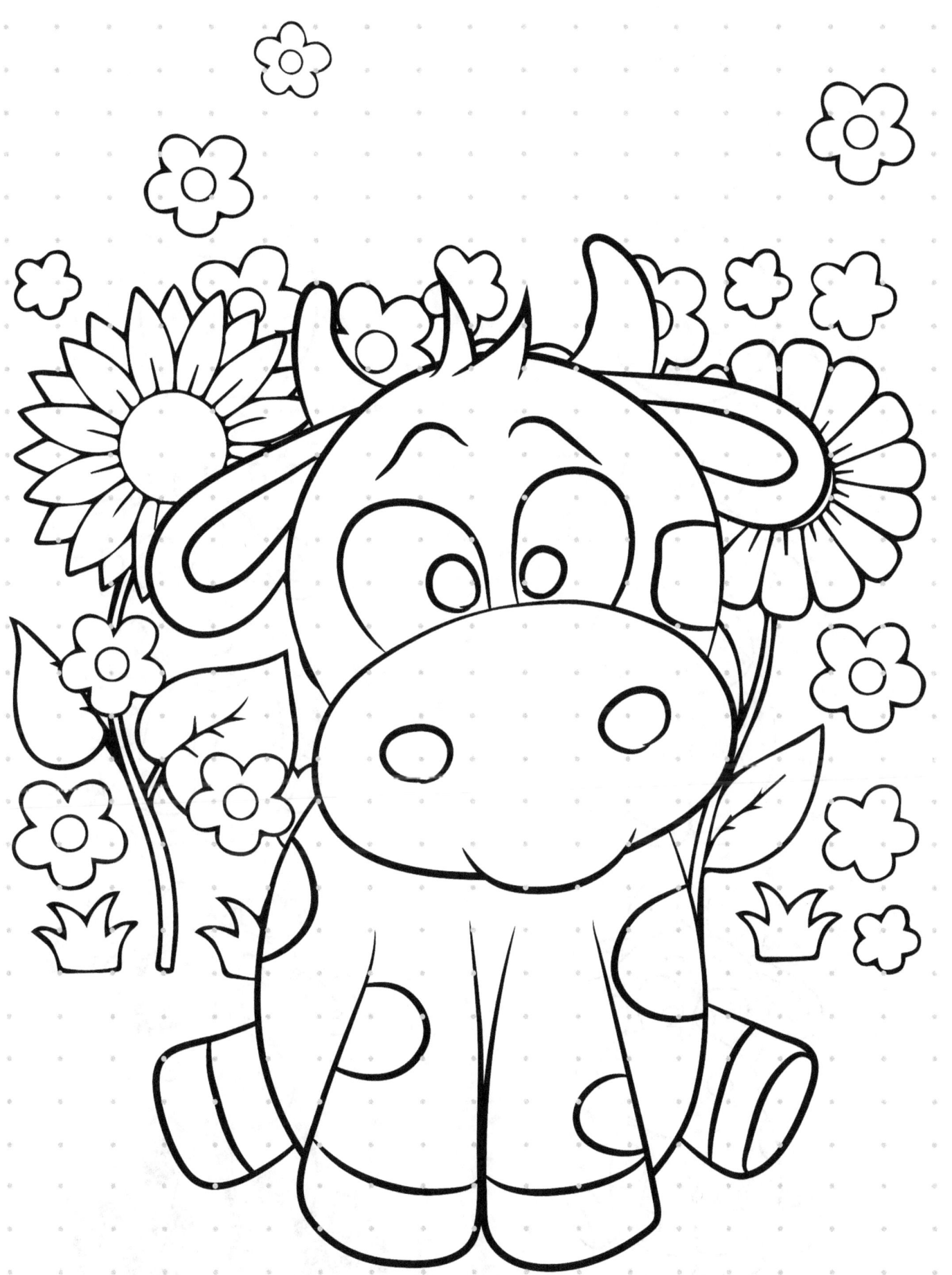

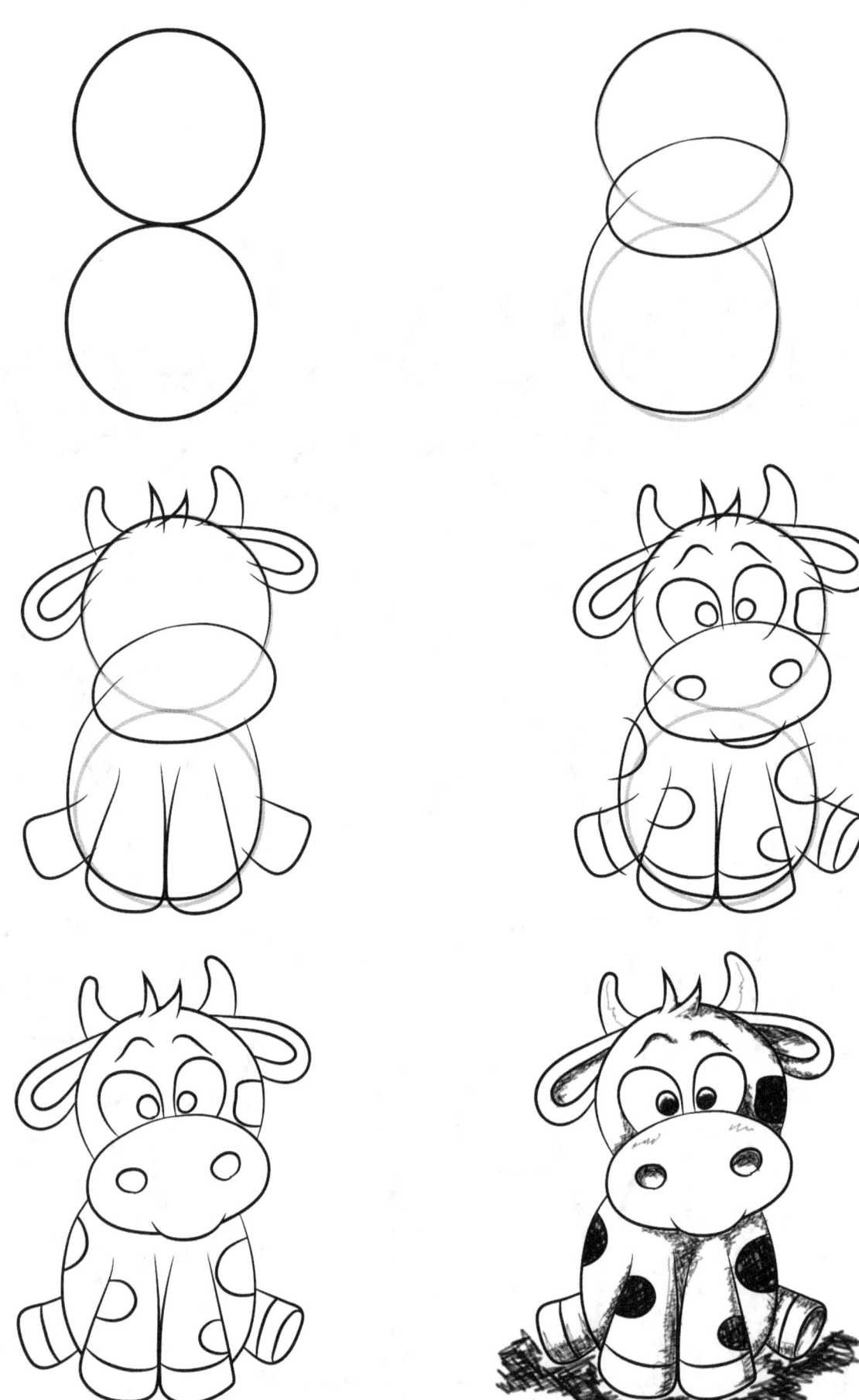

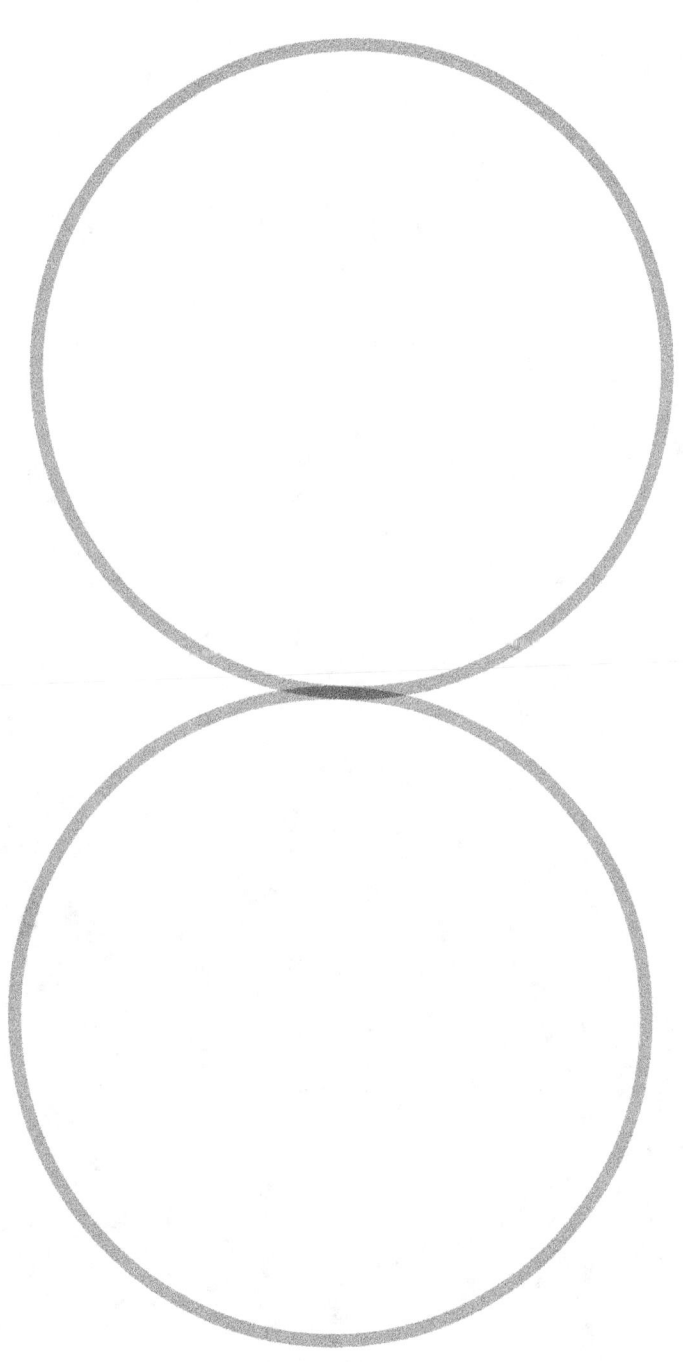

RABBIT
SIT

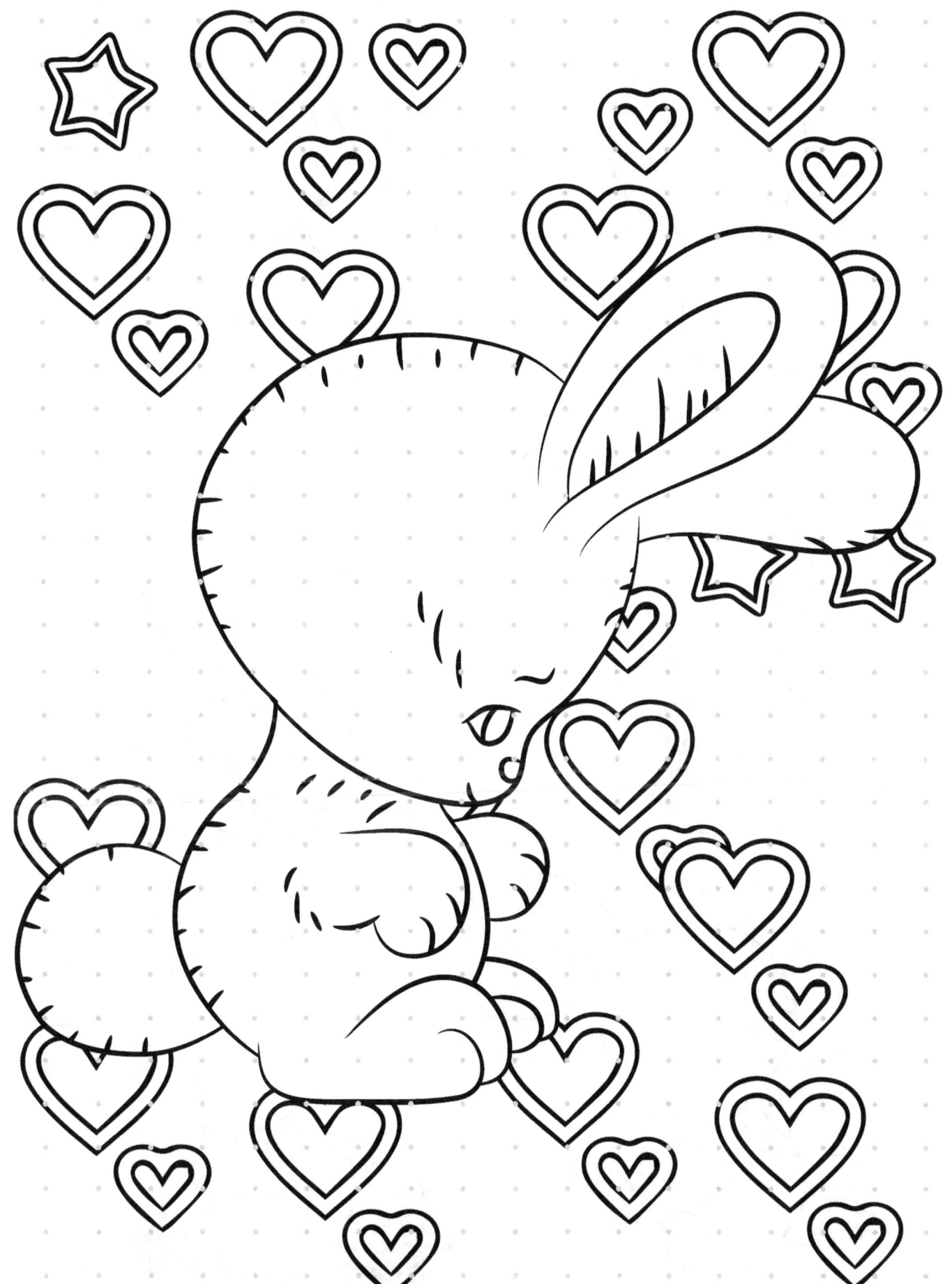

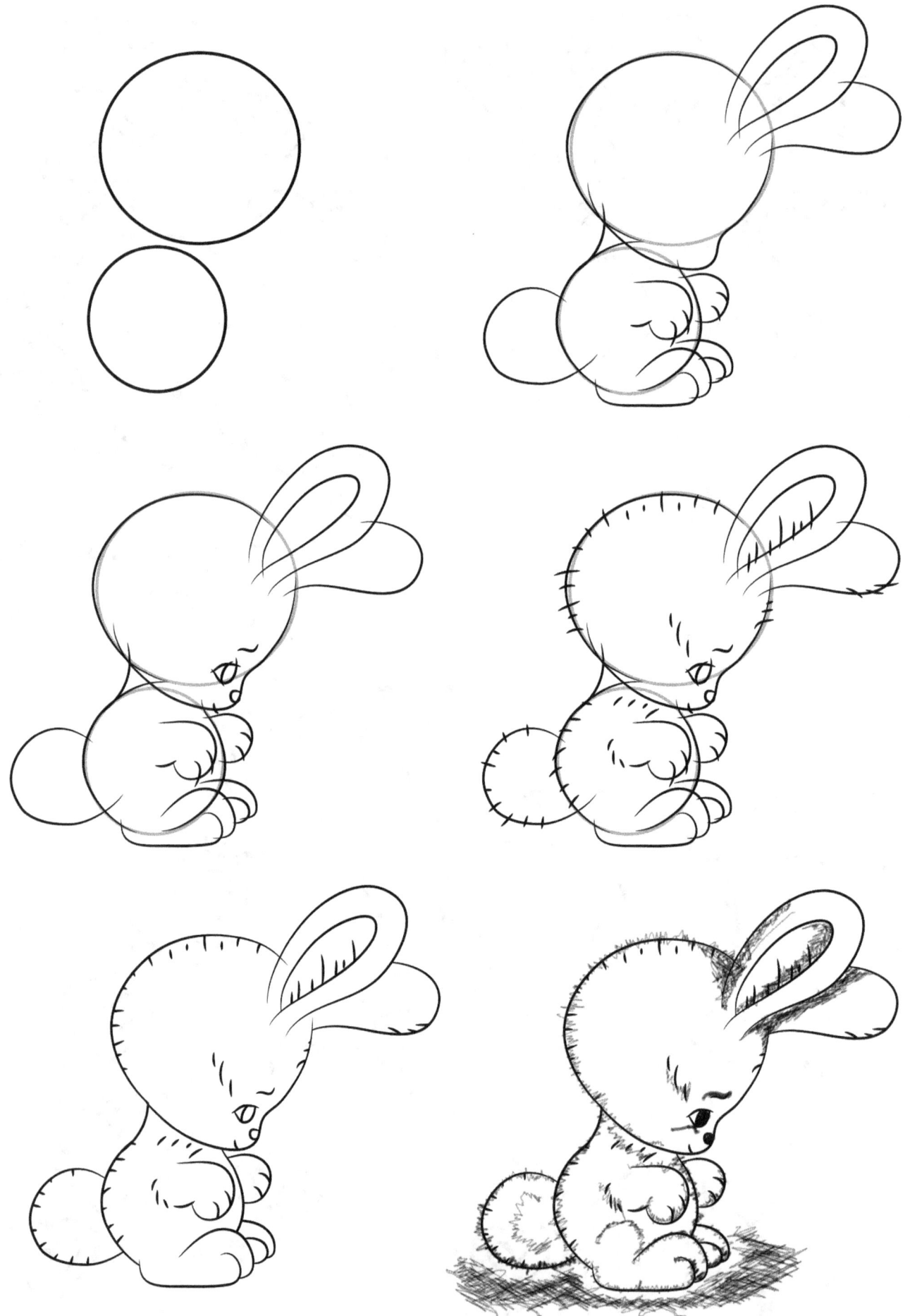

UNICORN
SIT

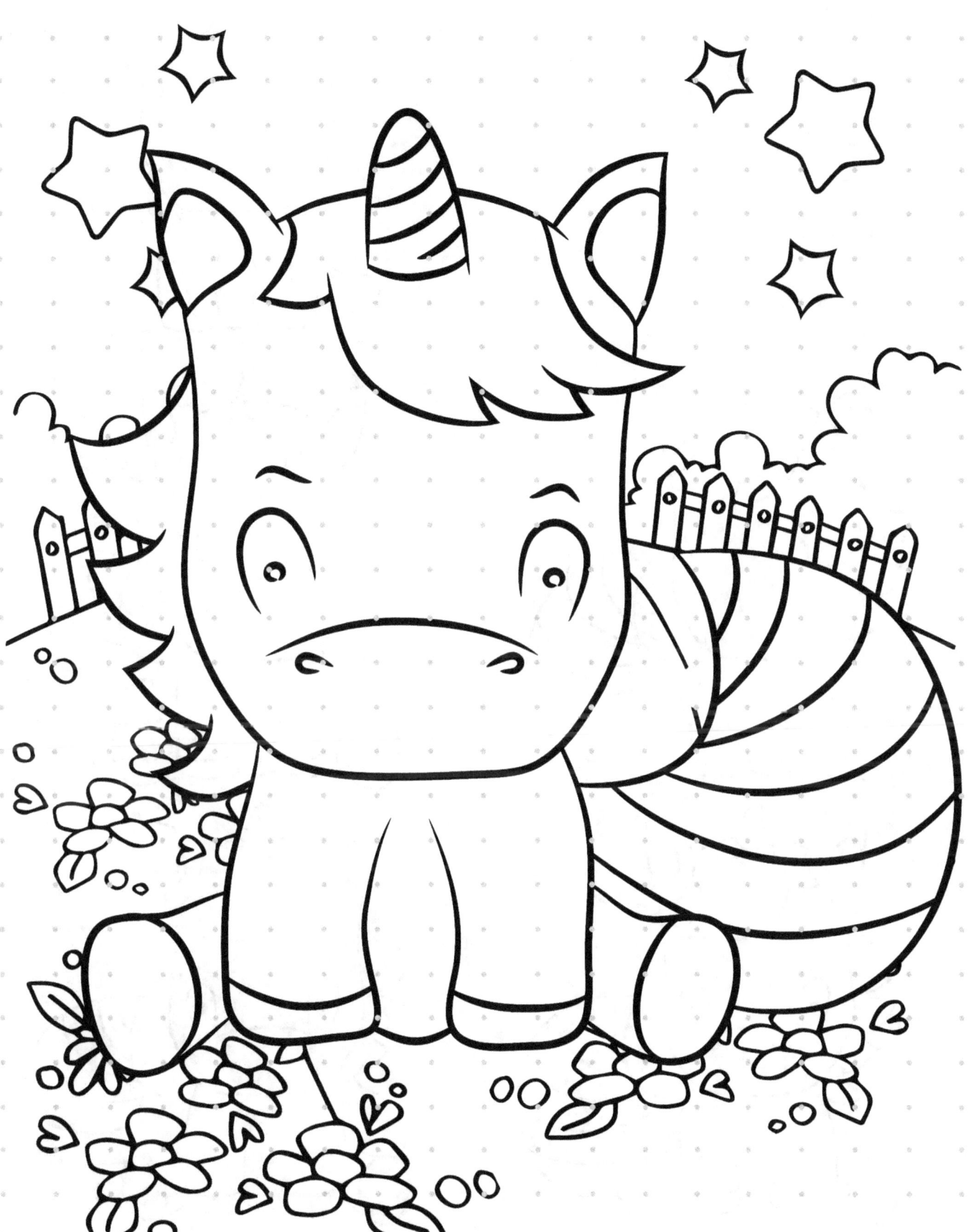

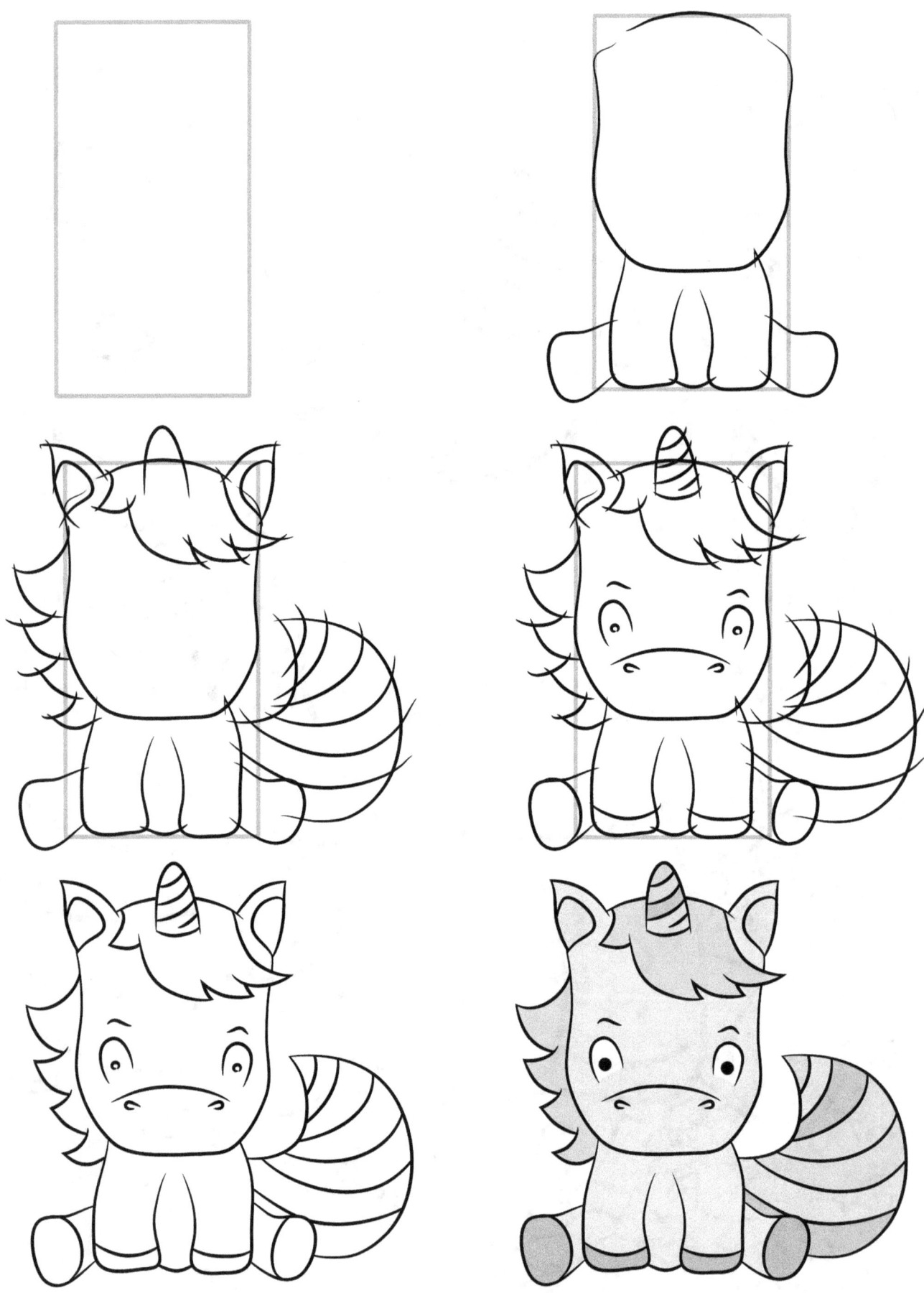

DEER
SLEEP

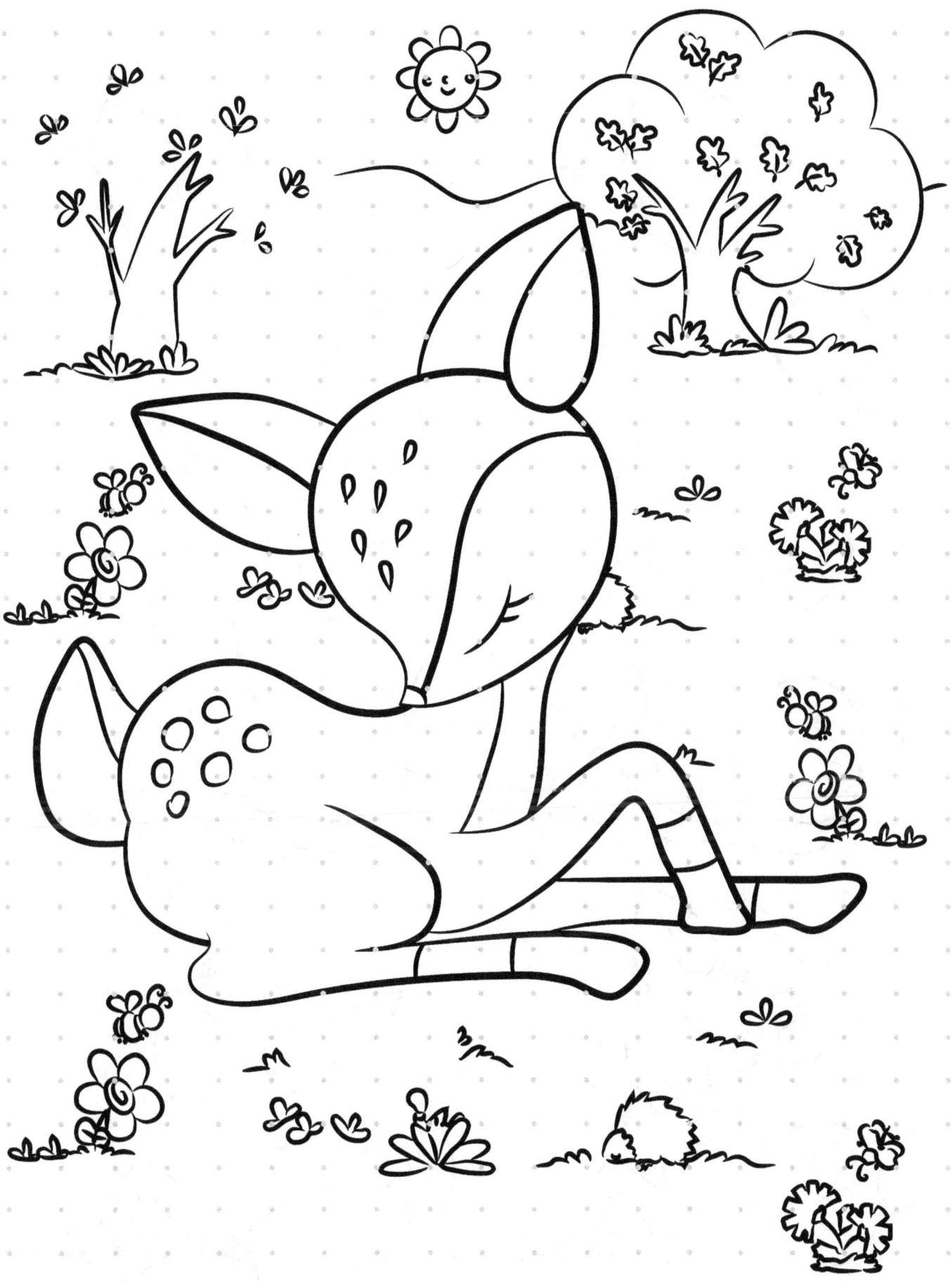

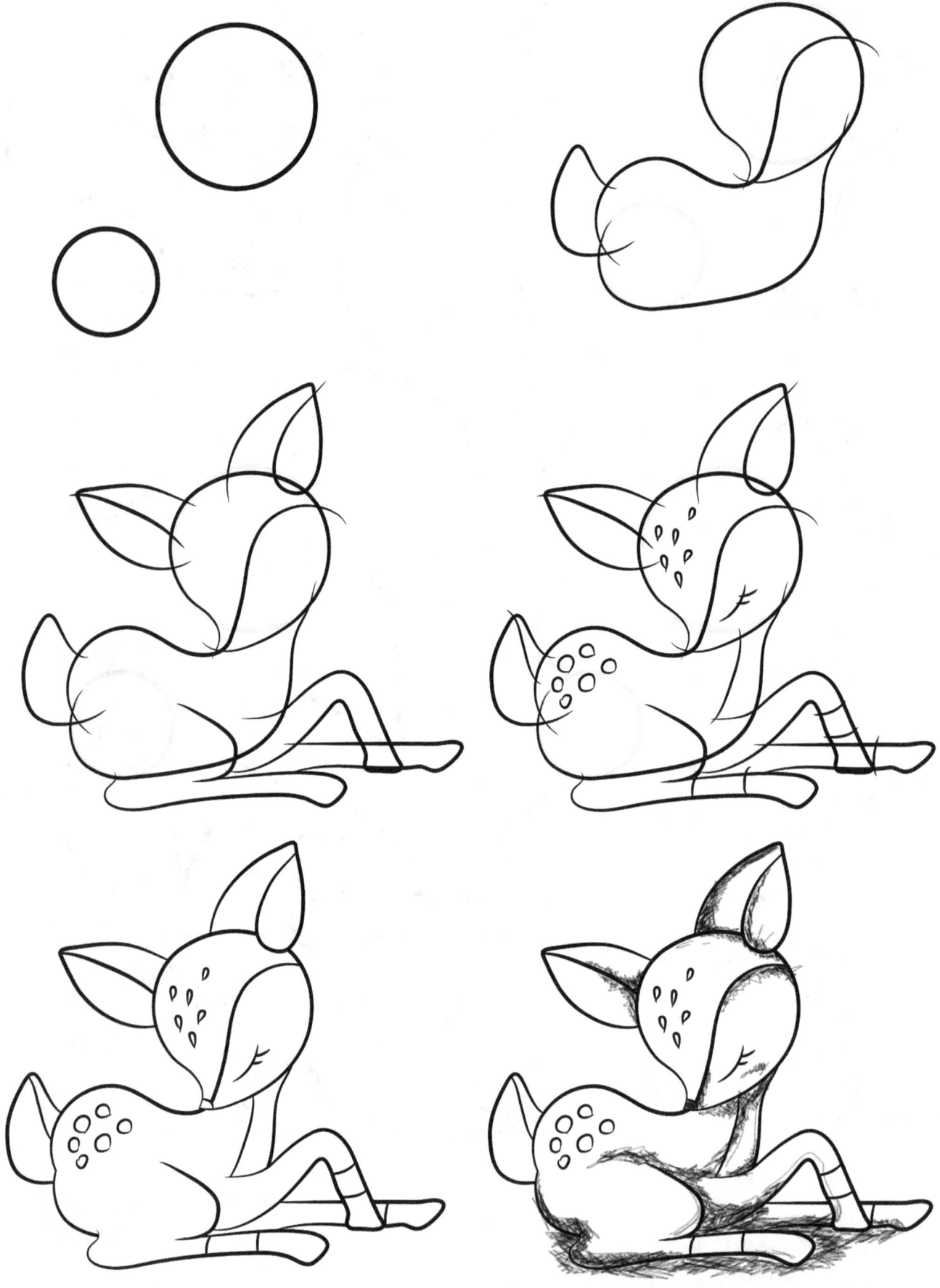

DEER
SLEEP

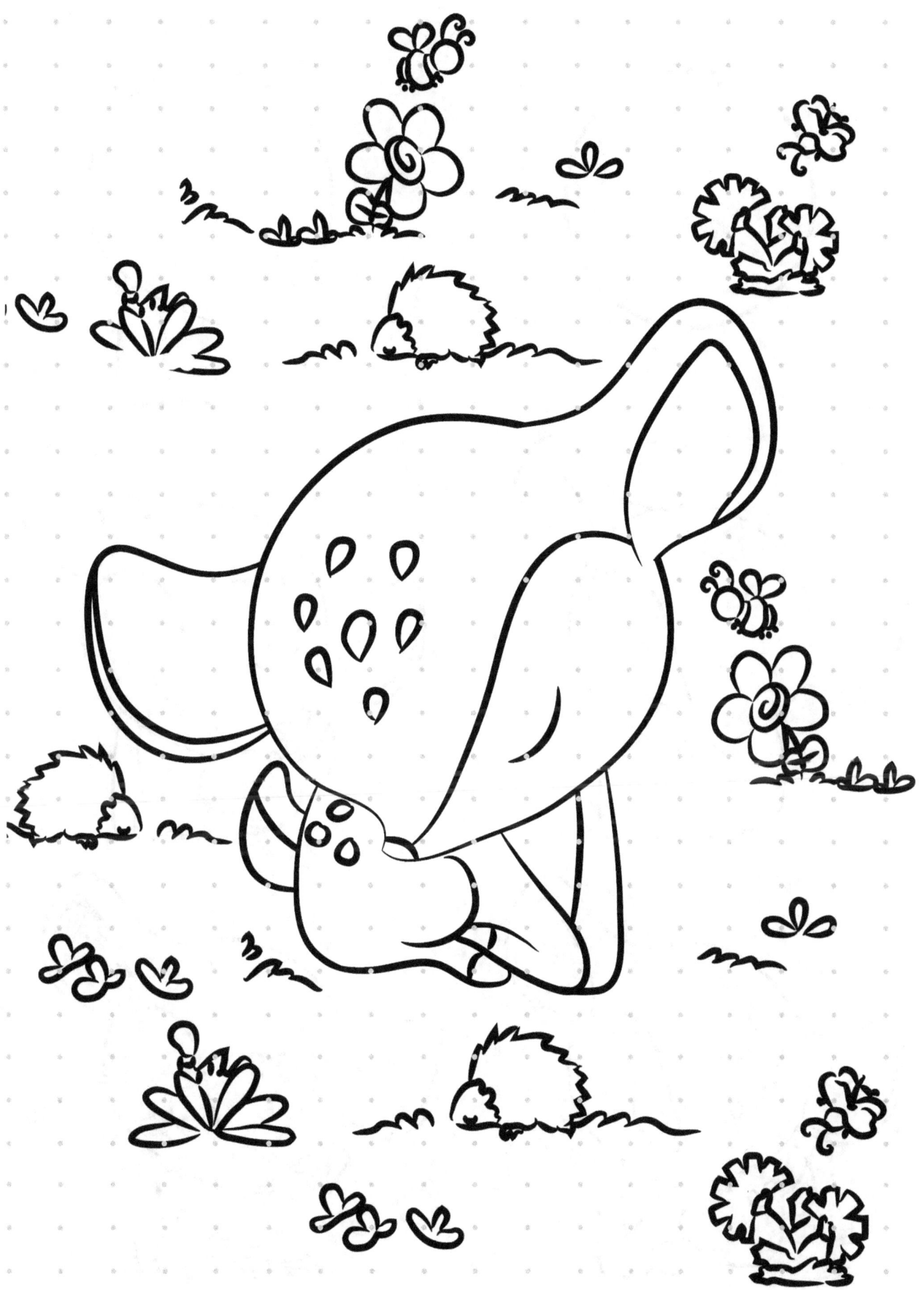

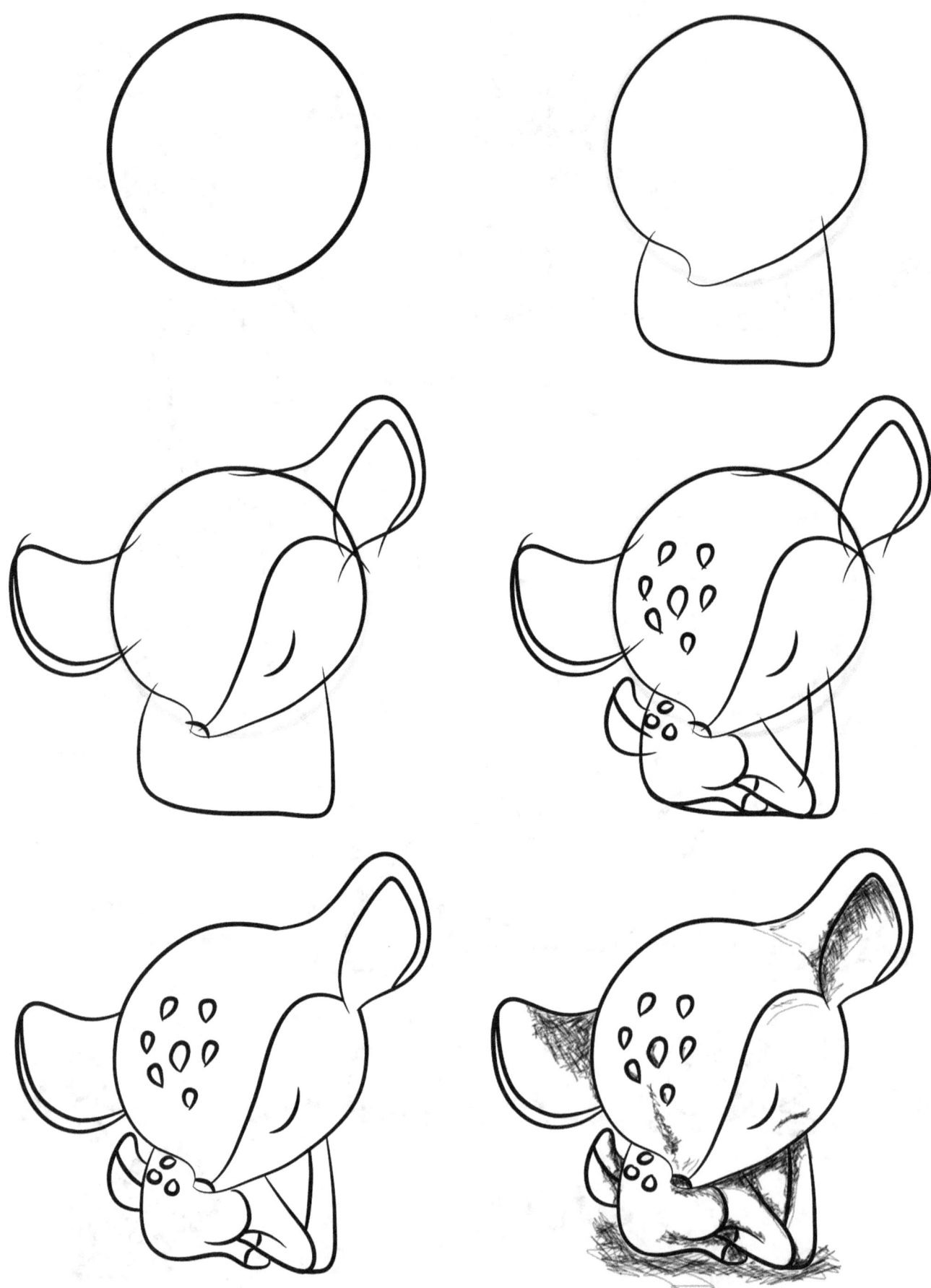

GIRAFFE
SIT

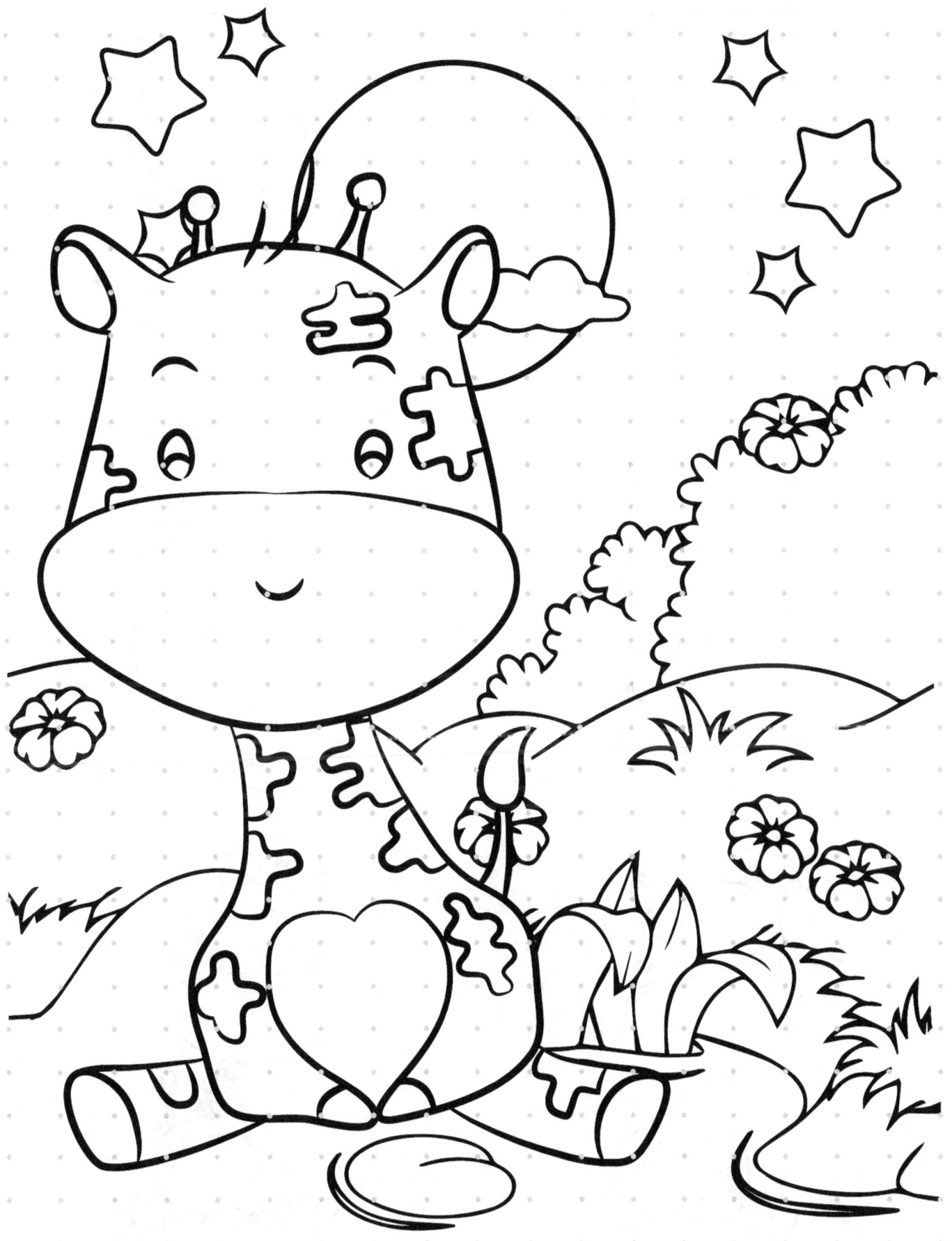

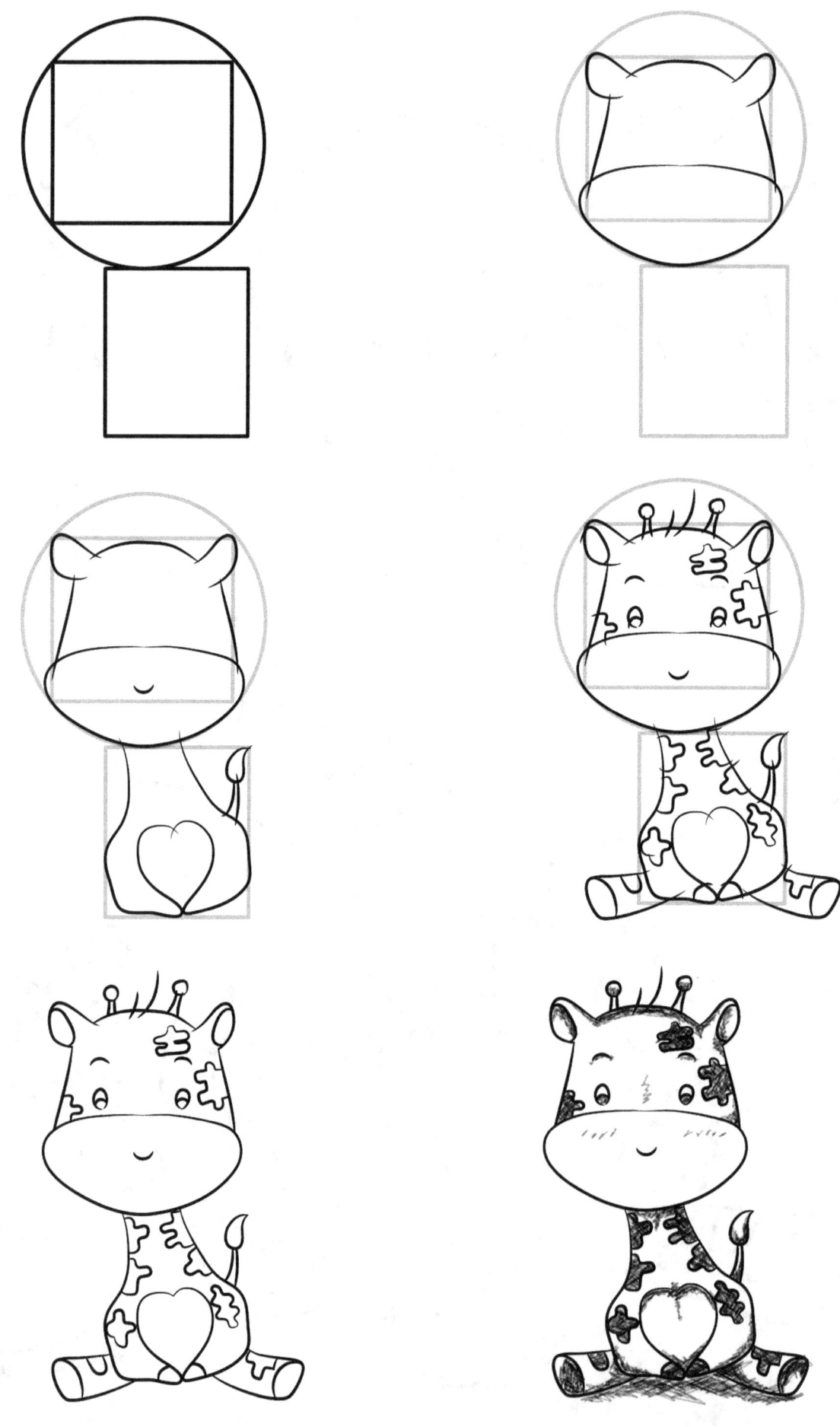

BEAR STAND

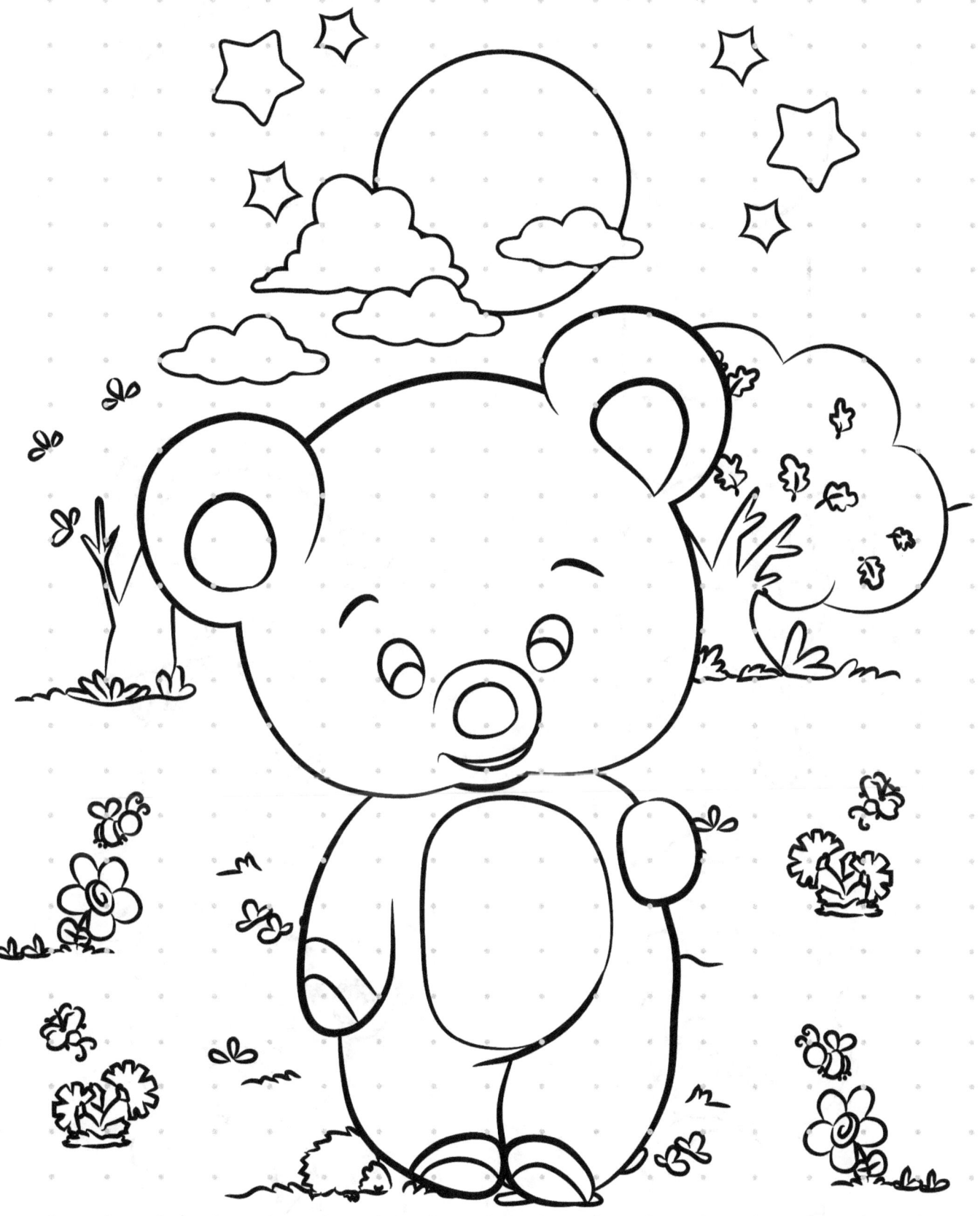

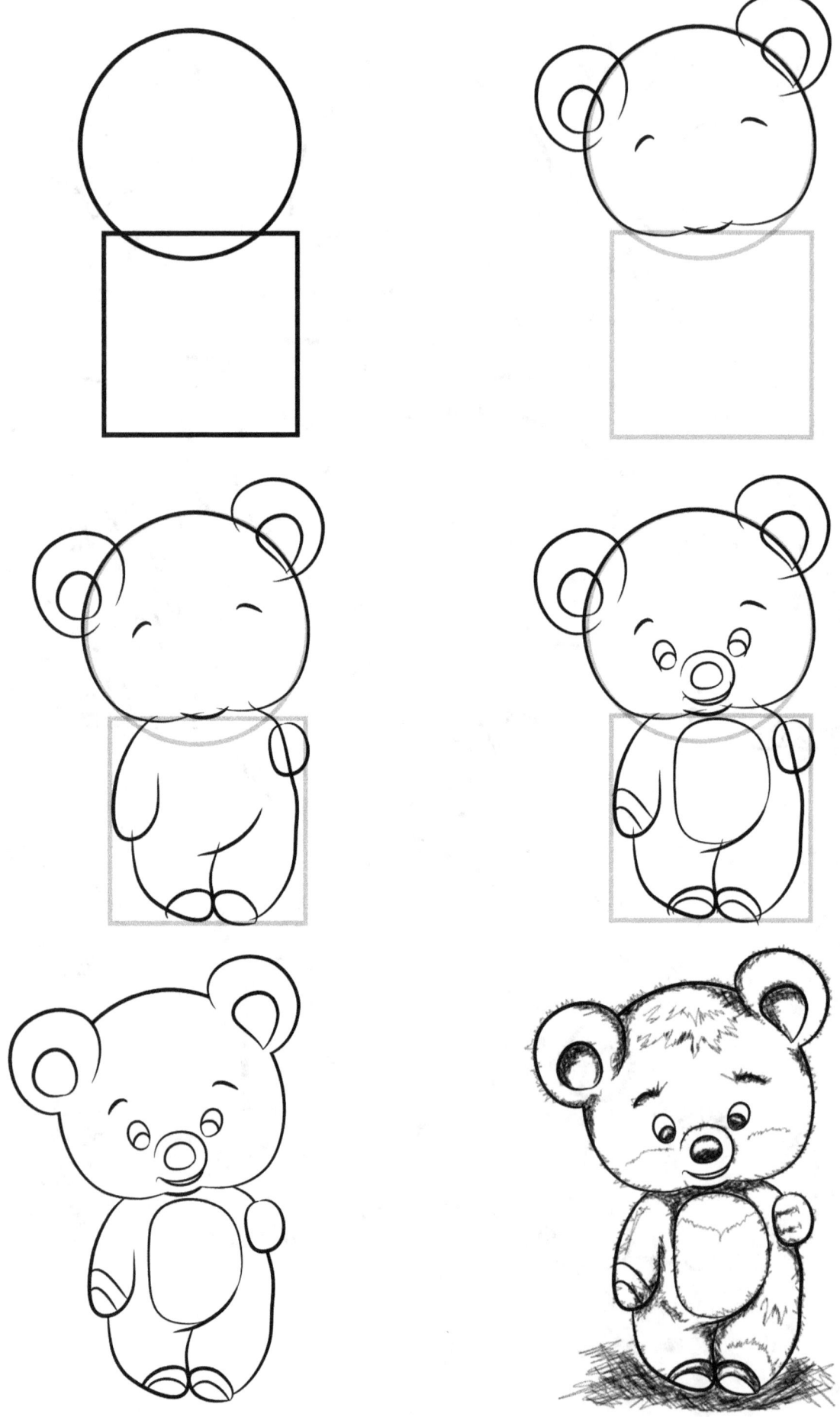

ELEPHANT

WALK

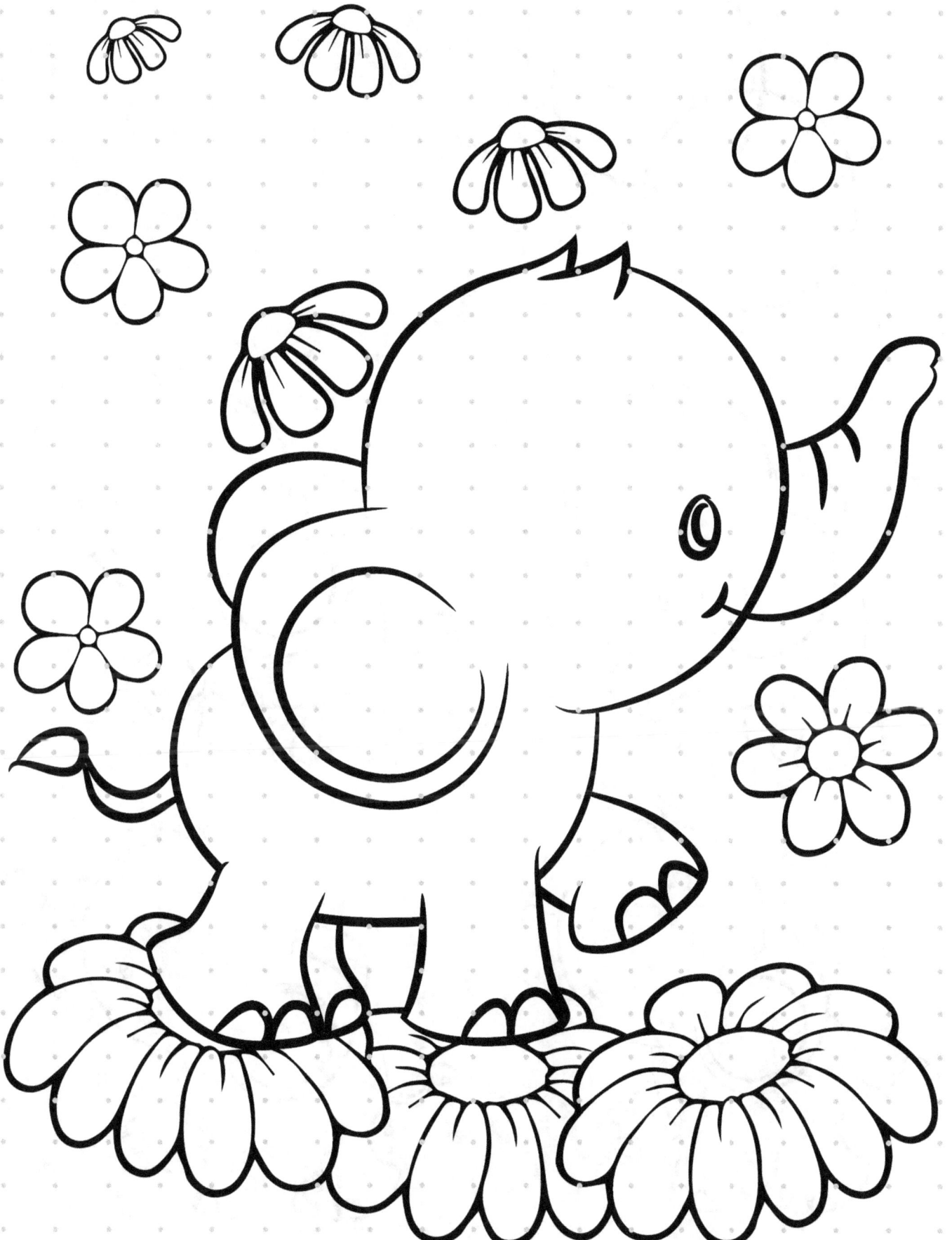

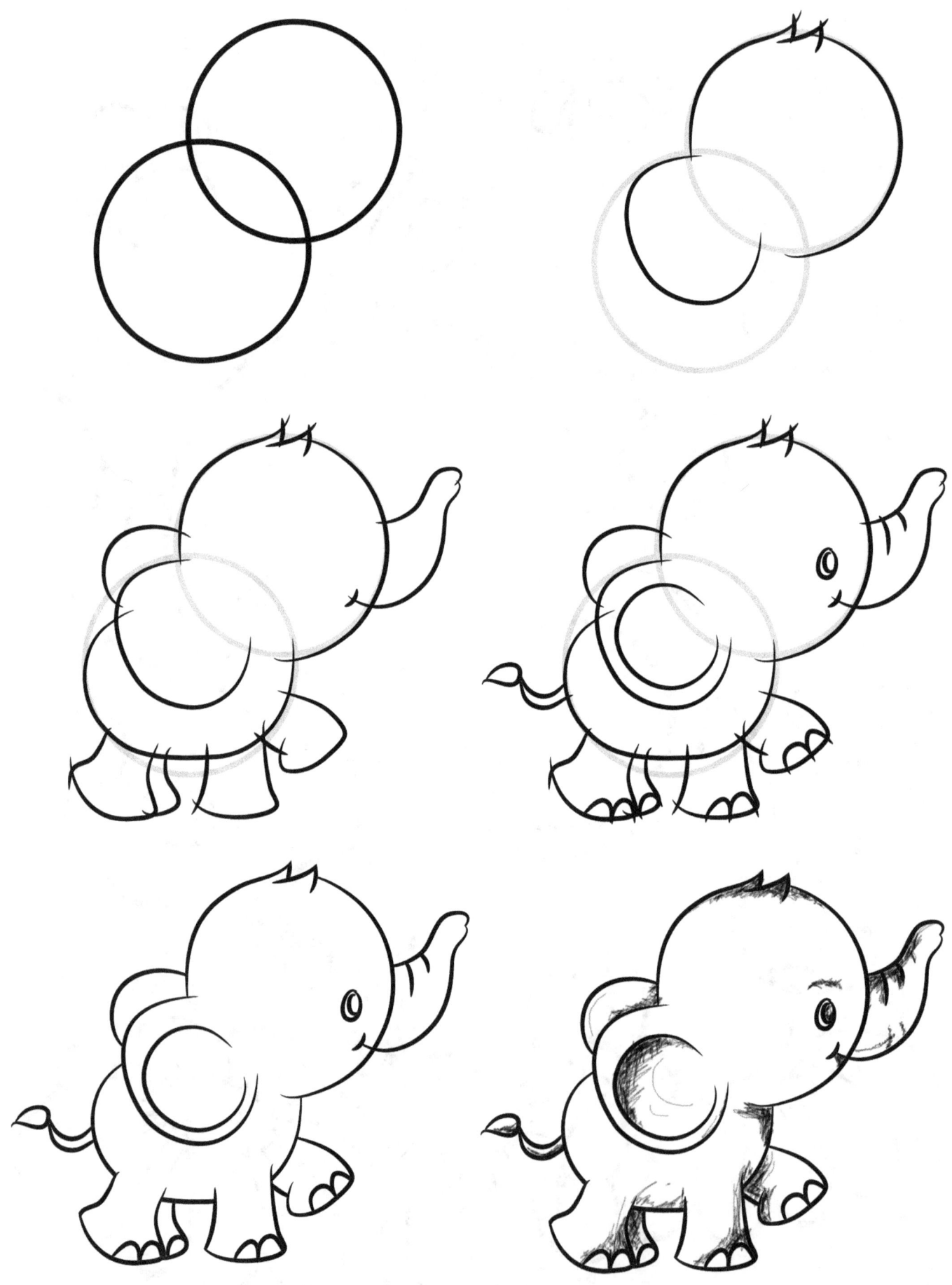

ELEPHANT
PLAY

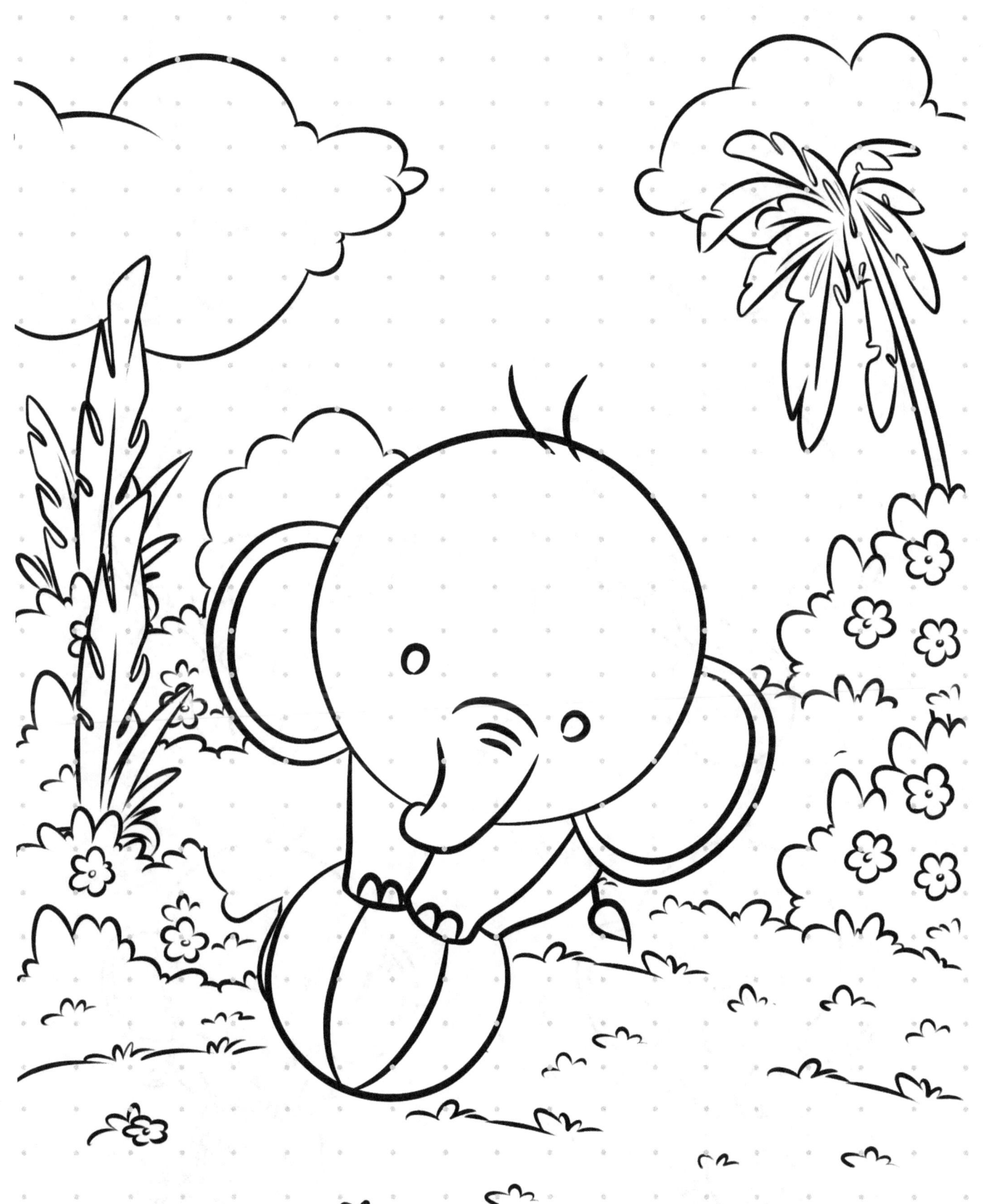

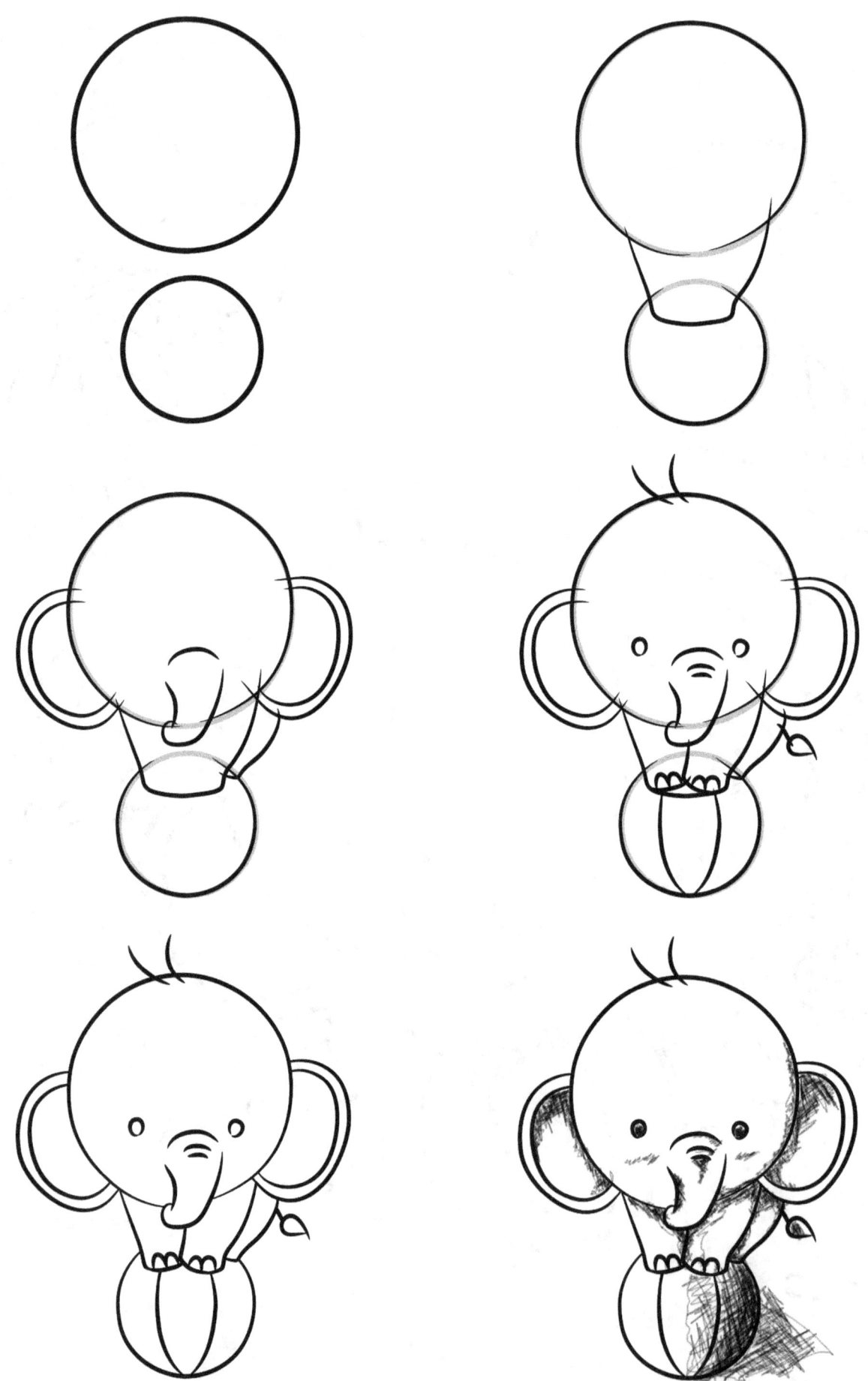

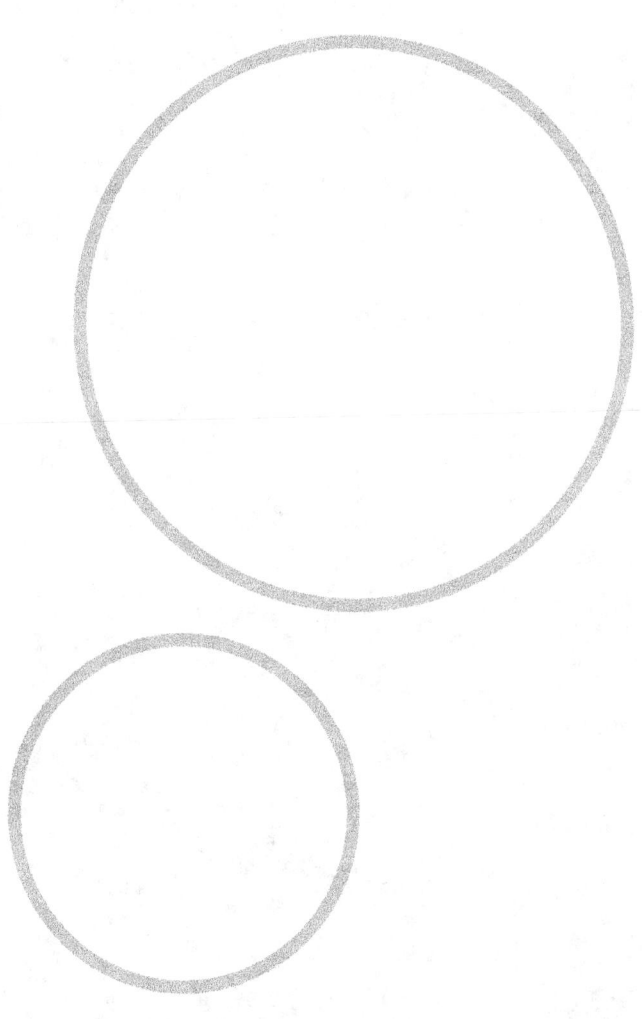

ELEPHANT
SIT

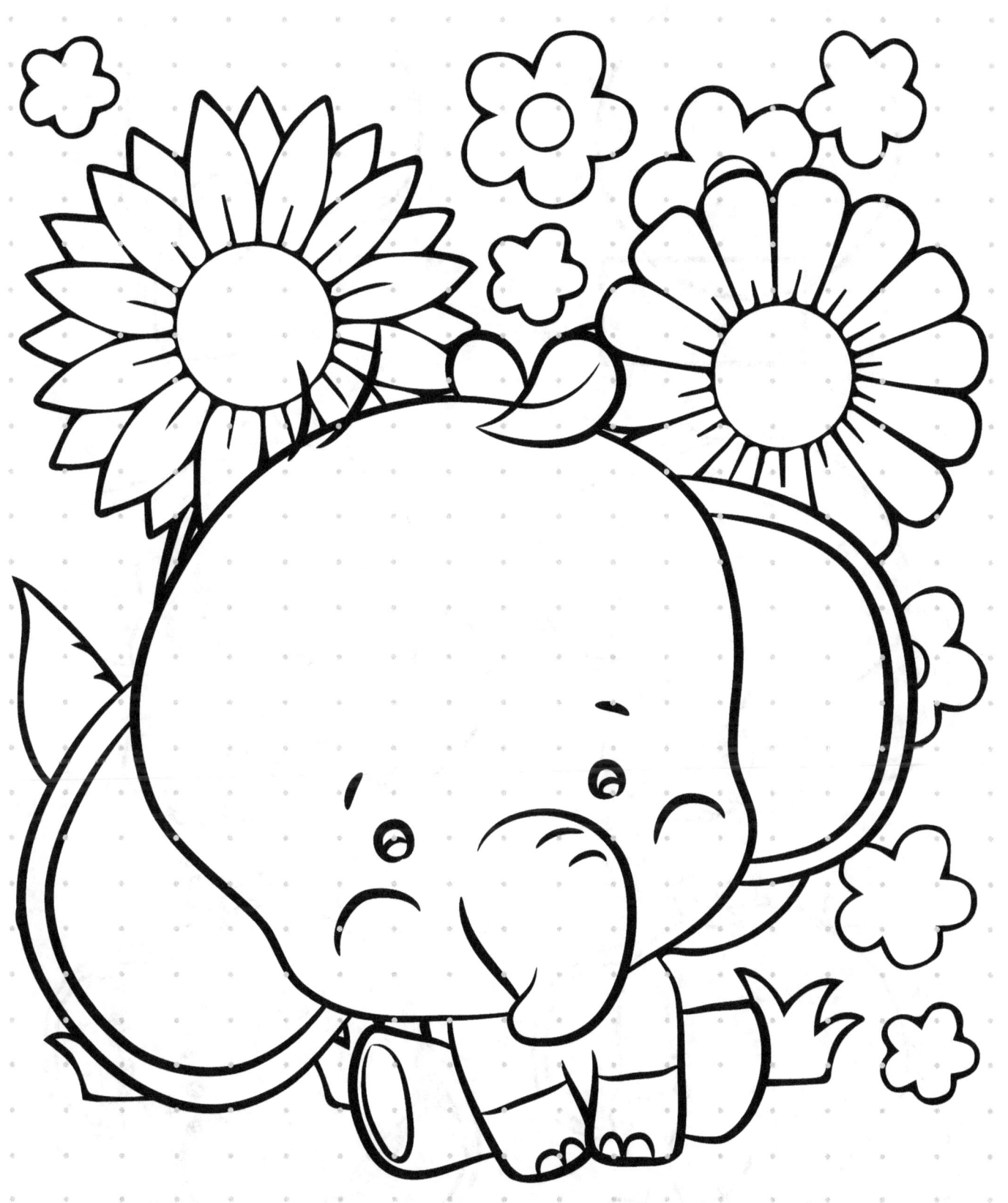

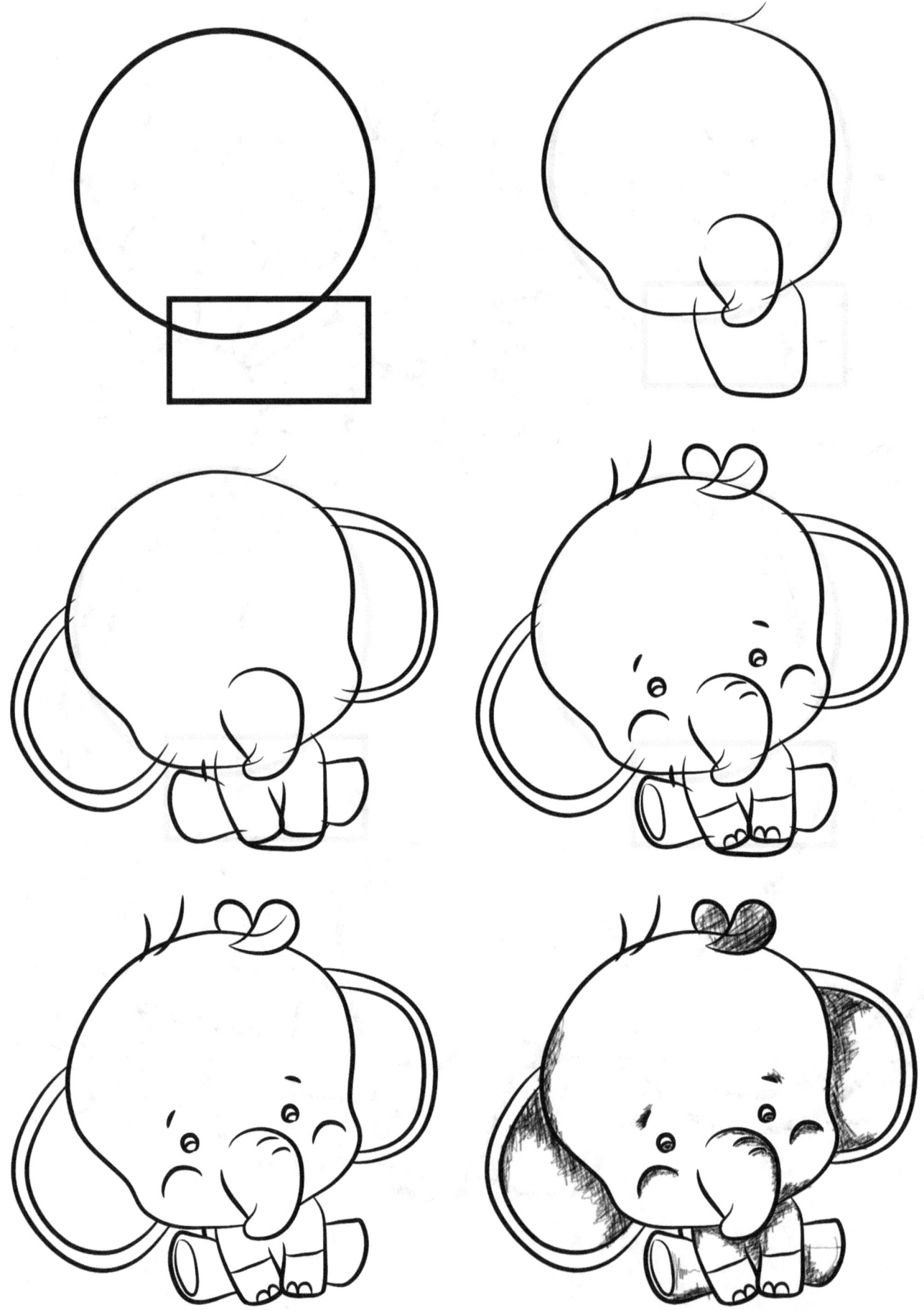

ELEPHANT
PLAY

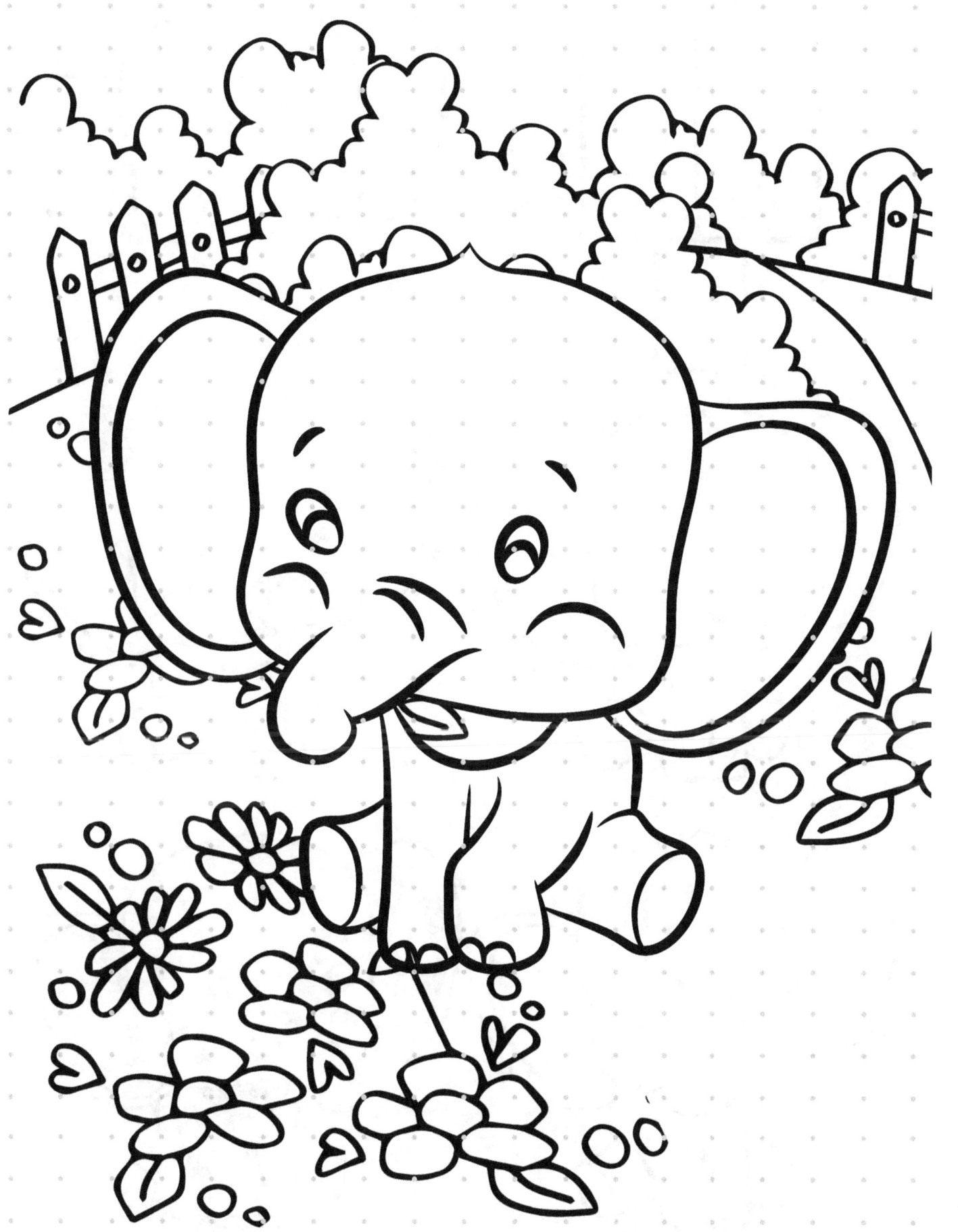

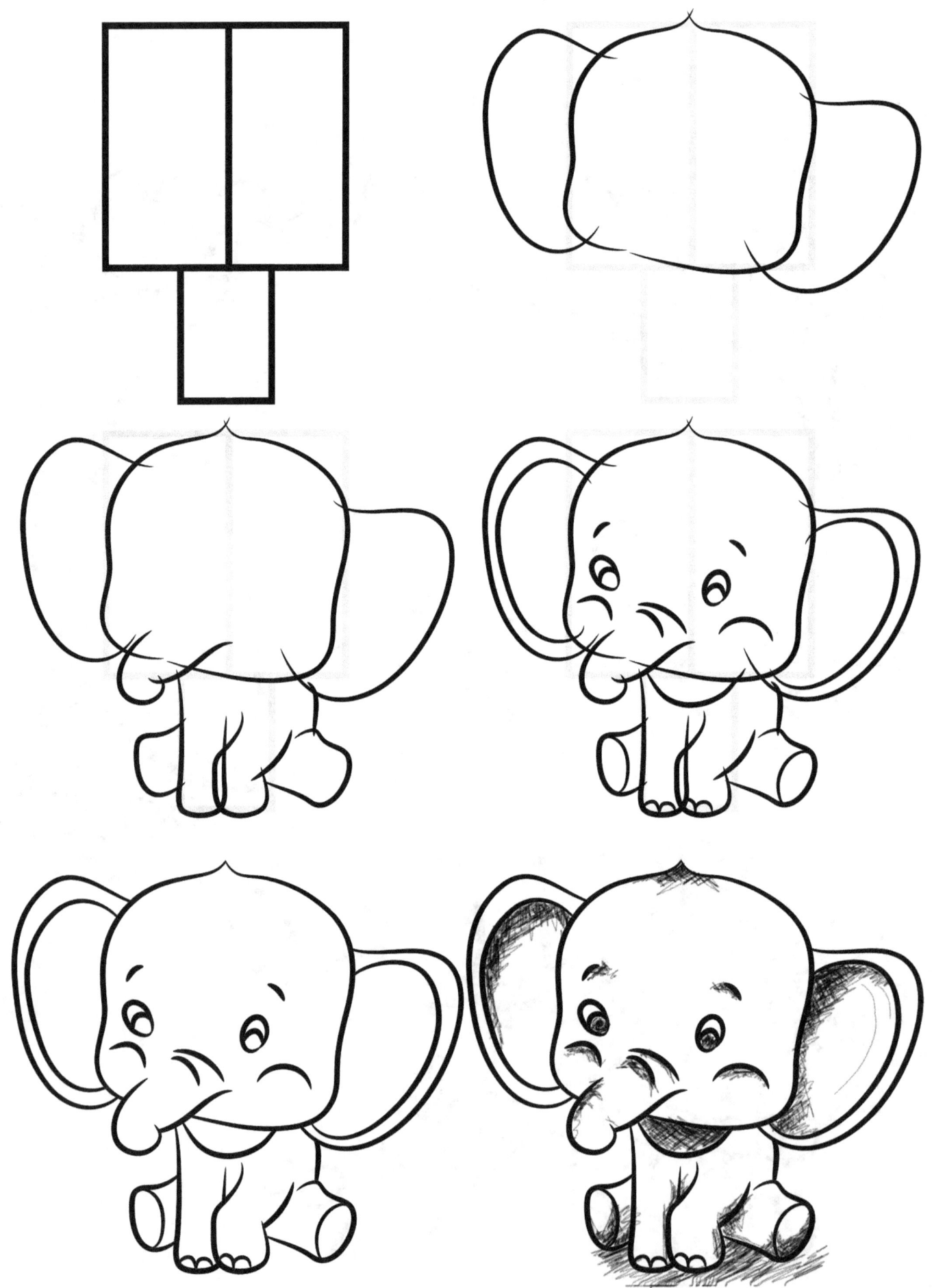

ELEPHANT

SIT

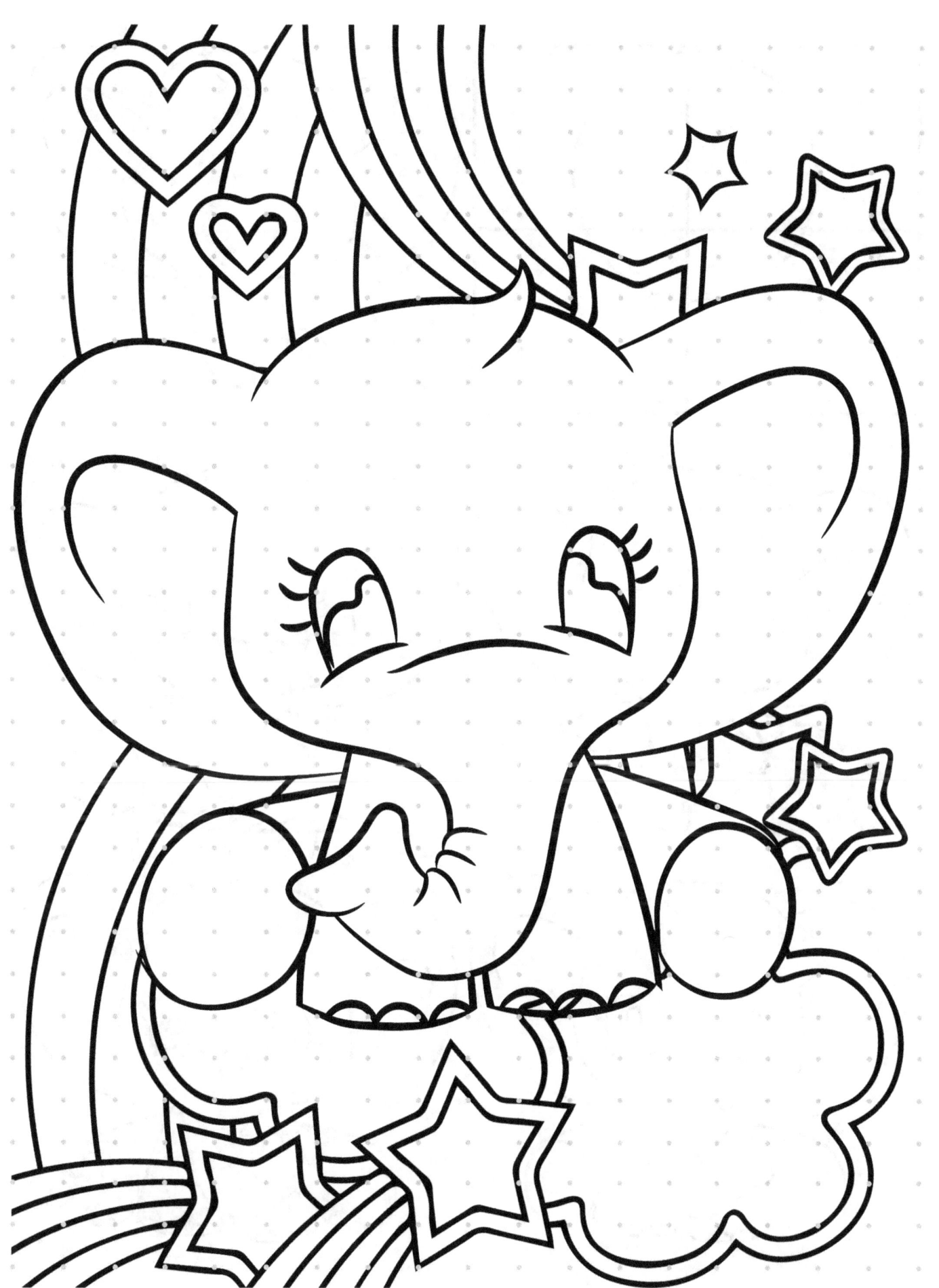

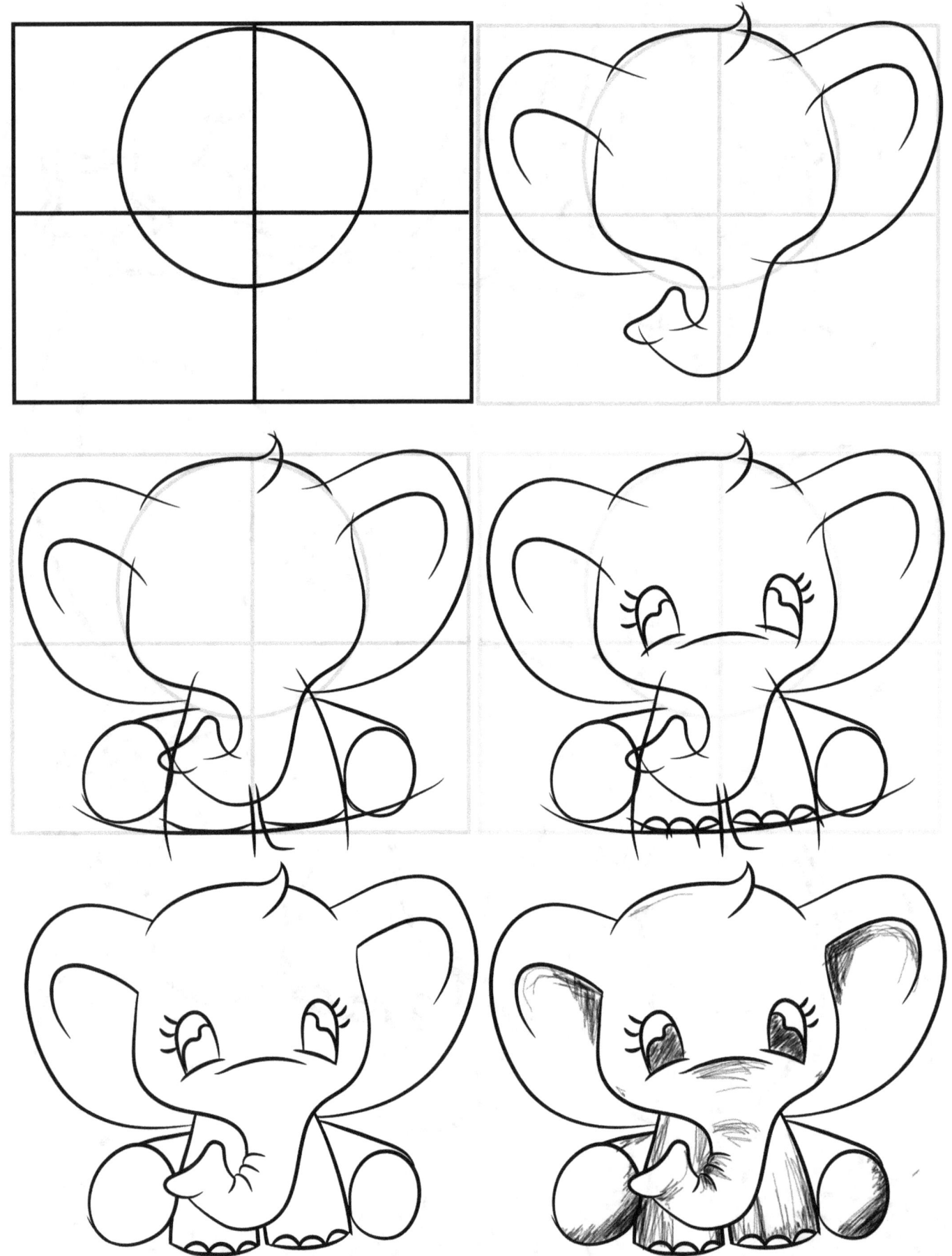

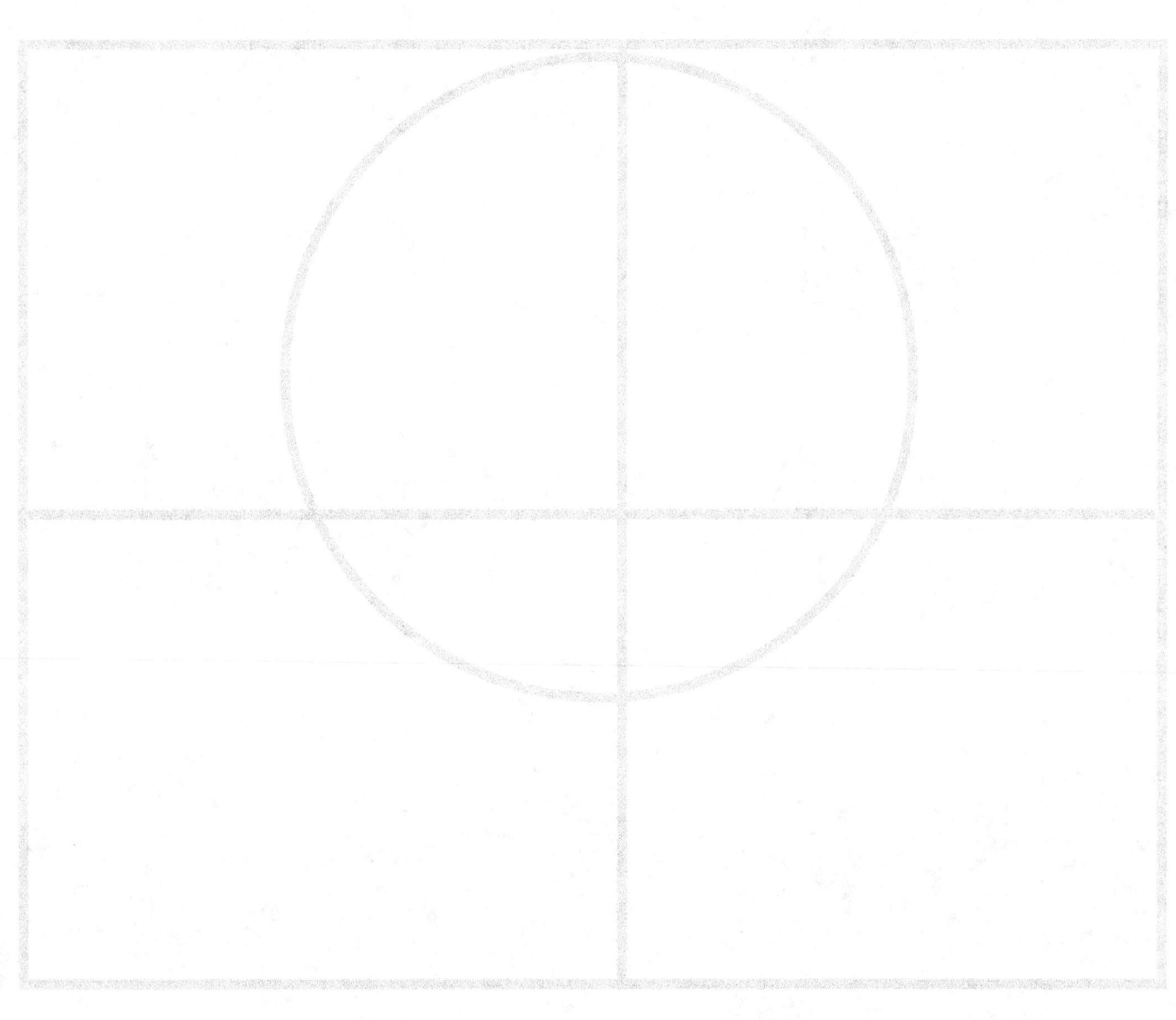

LION
SIT

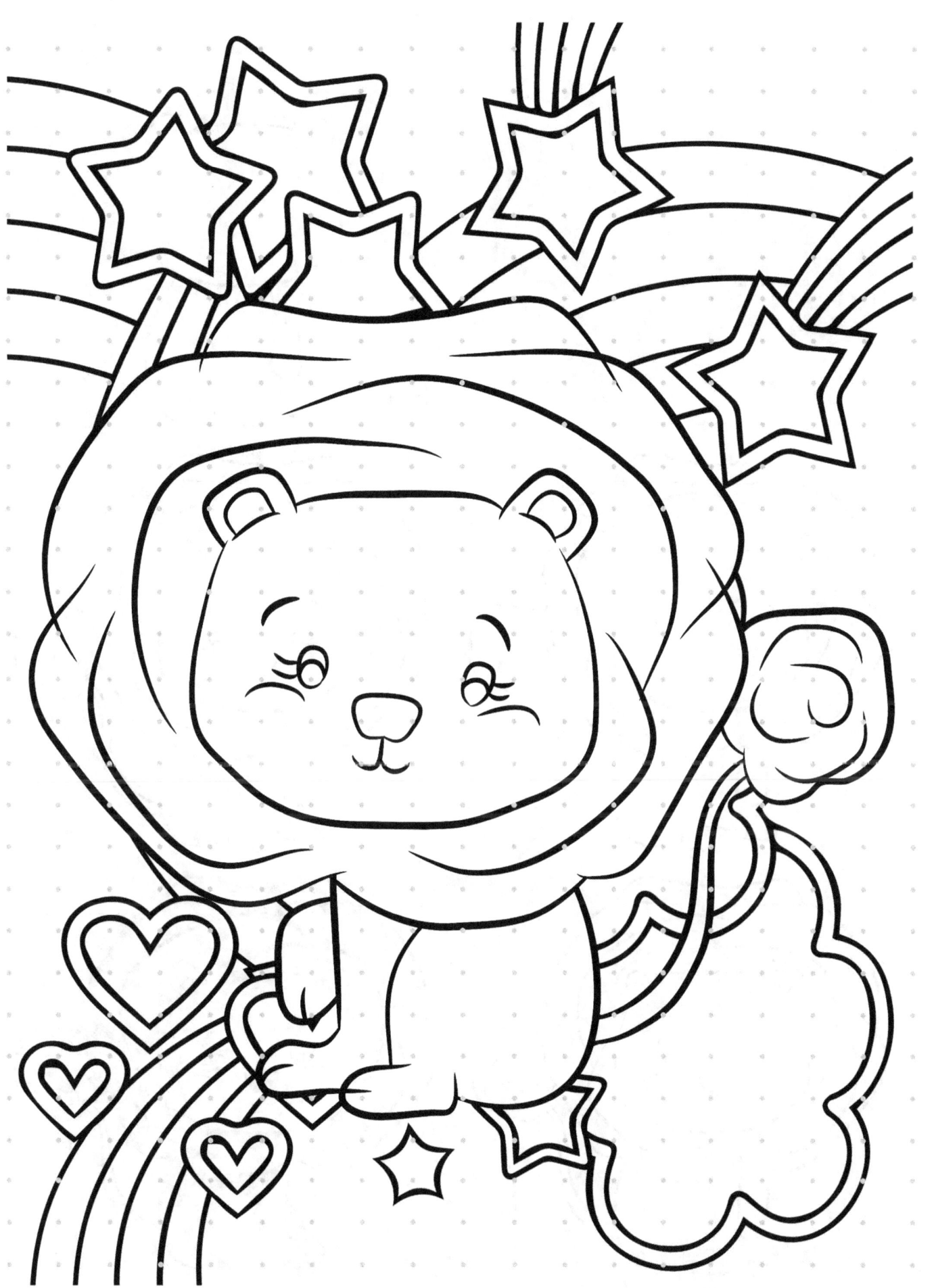

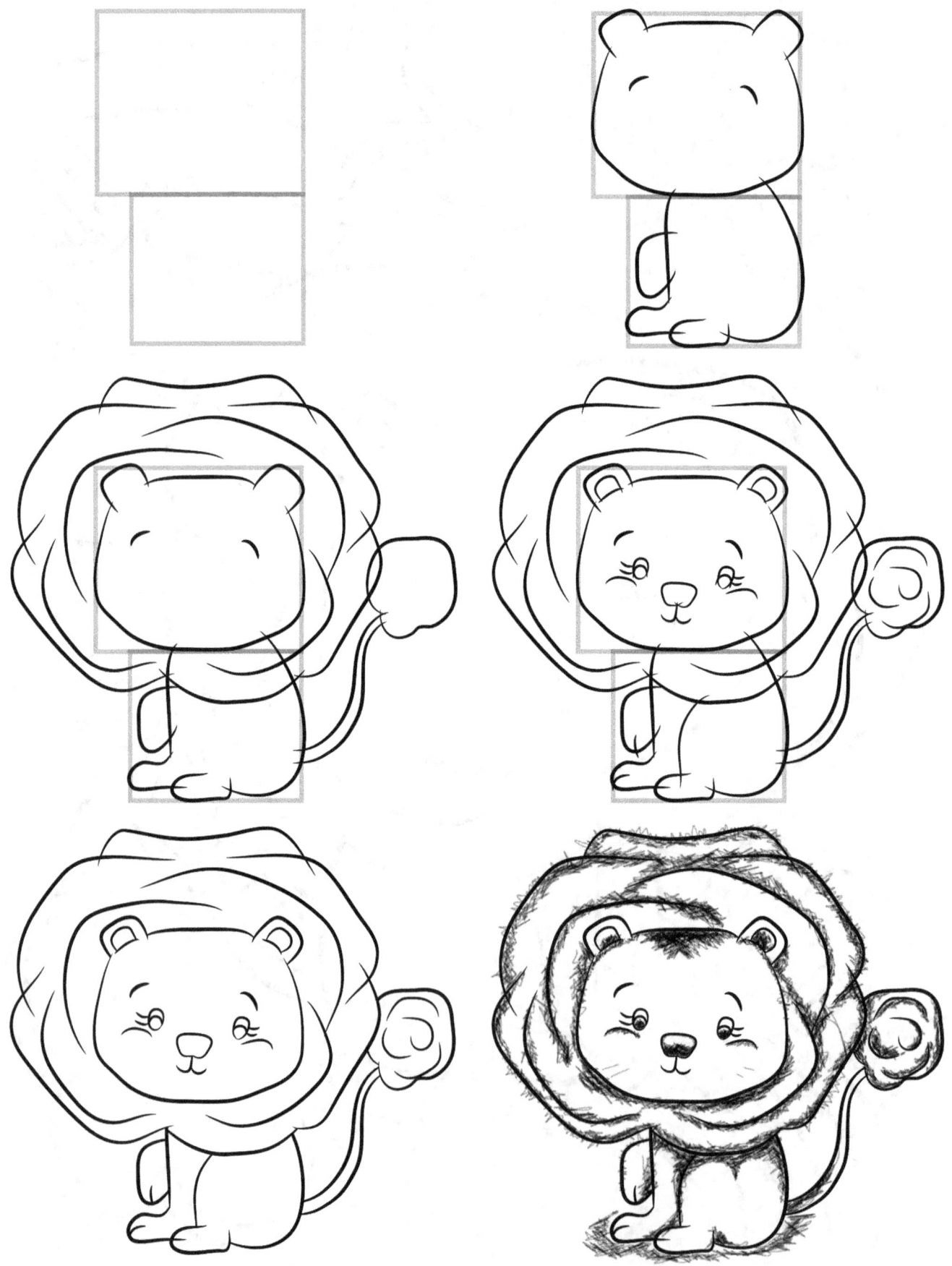

BEAR
PLAY

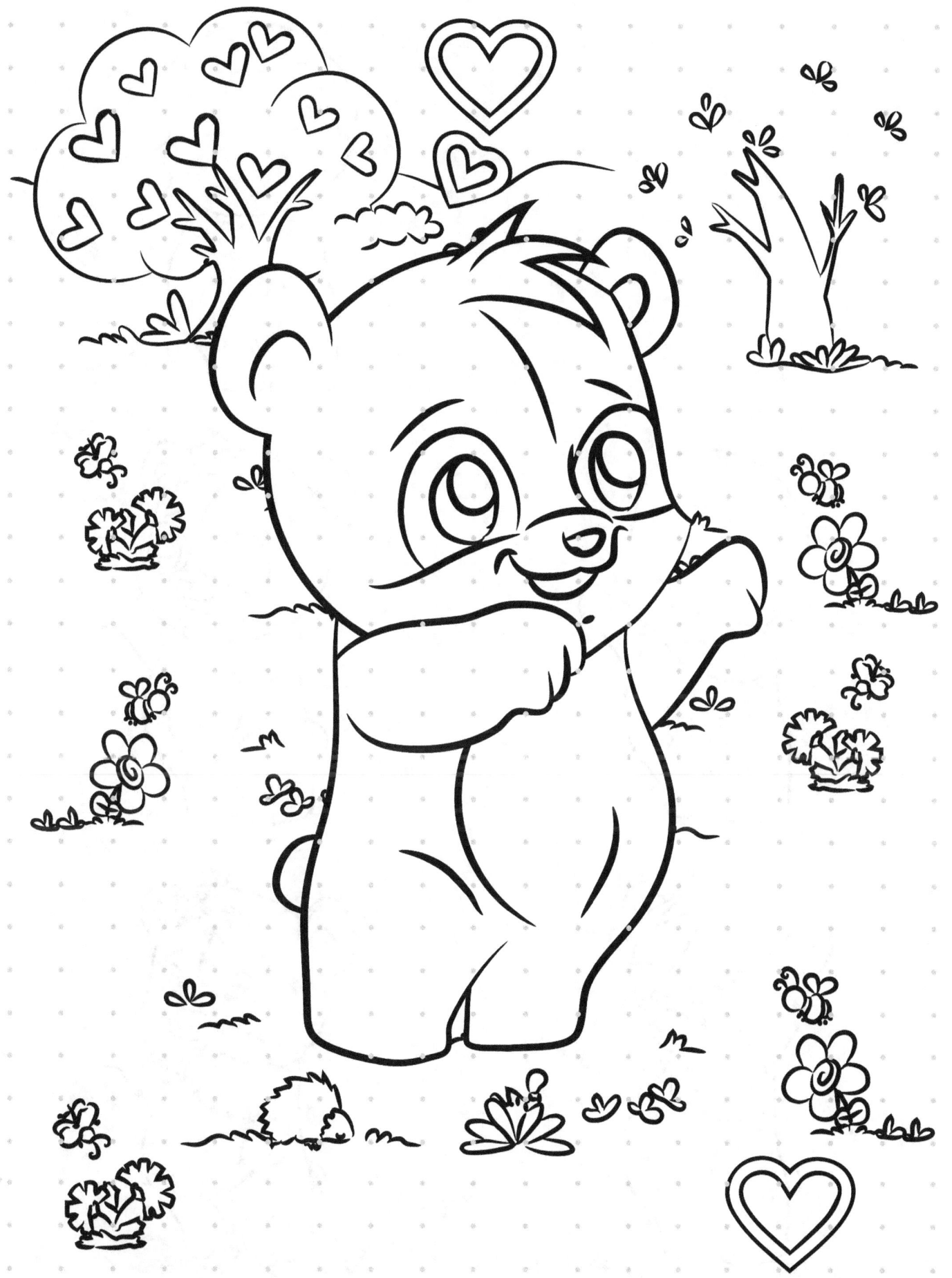

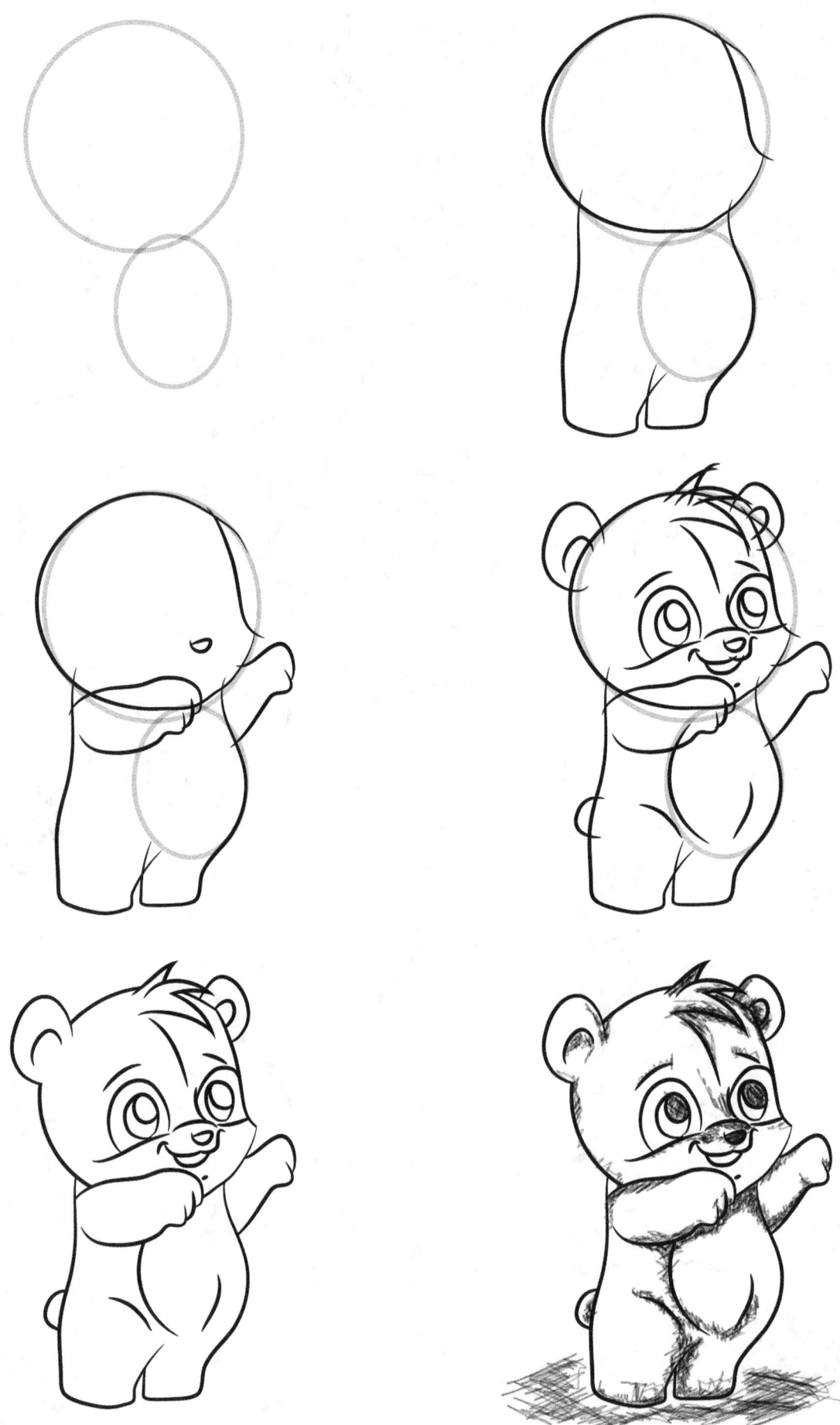

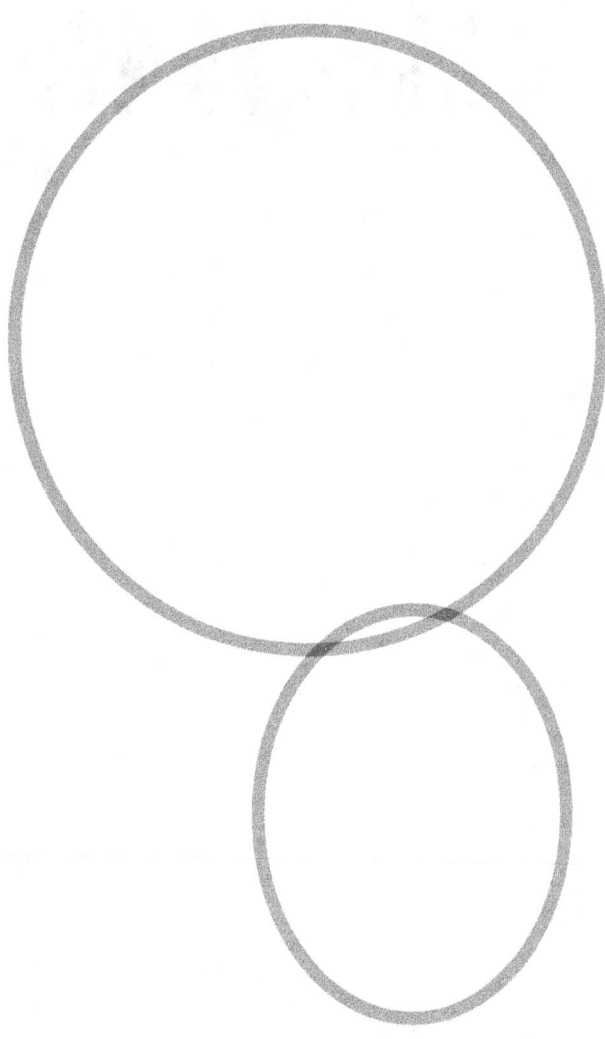

PENGUIN
STAND

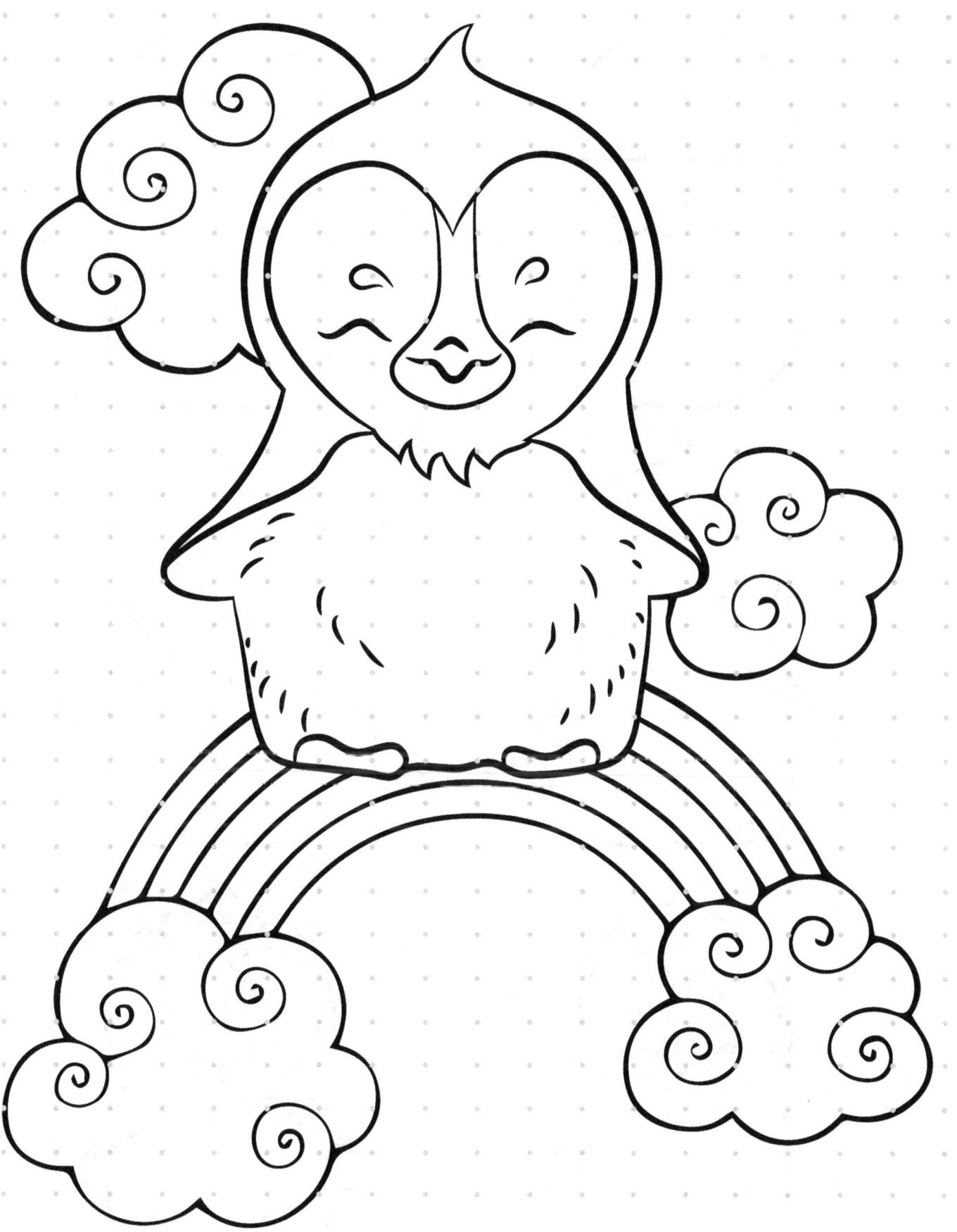

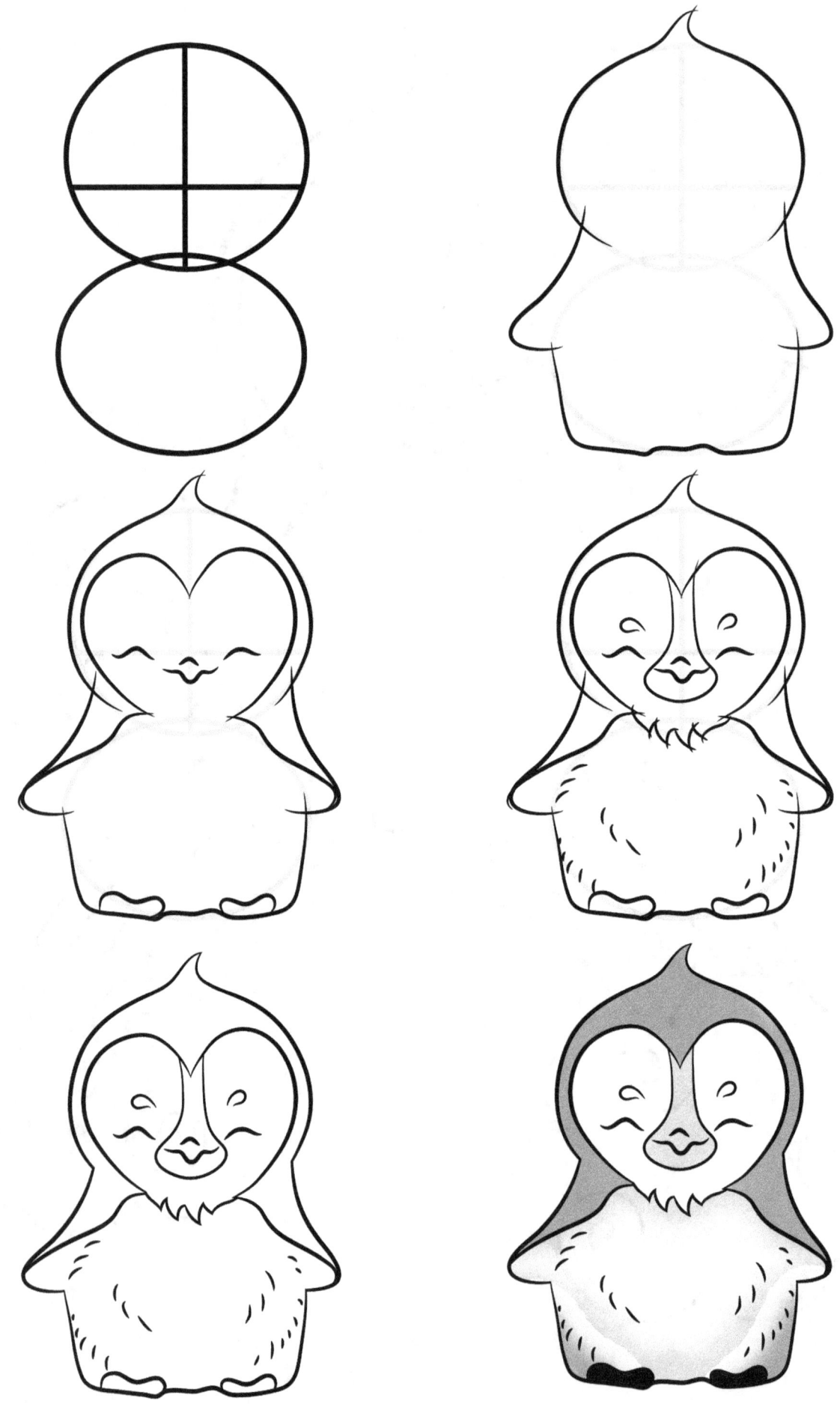

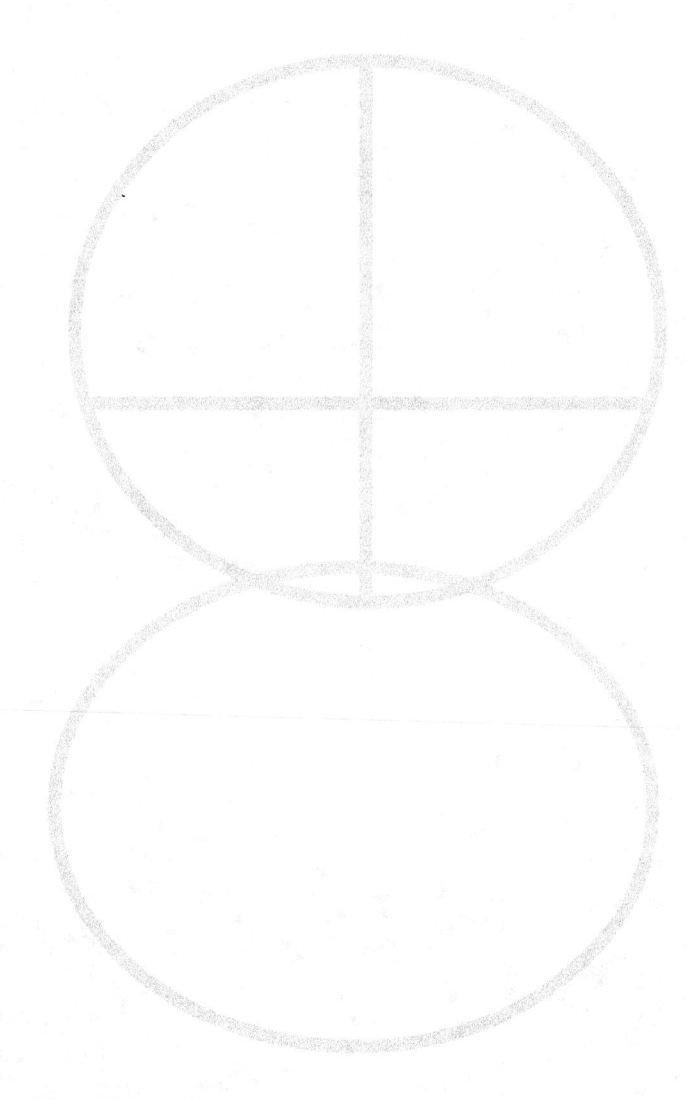

WHALE PLAY

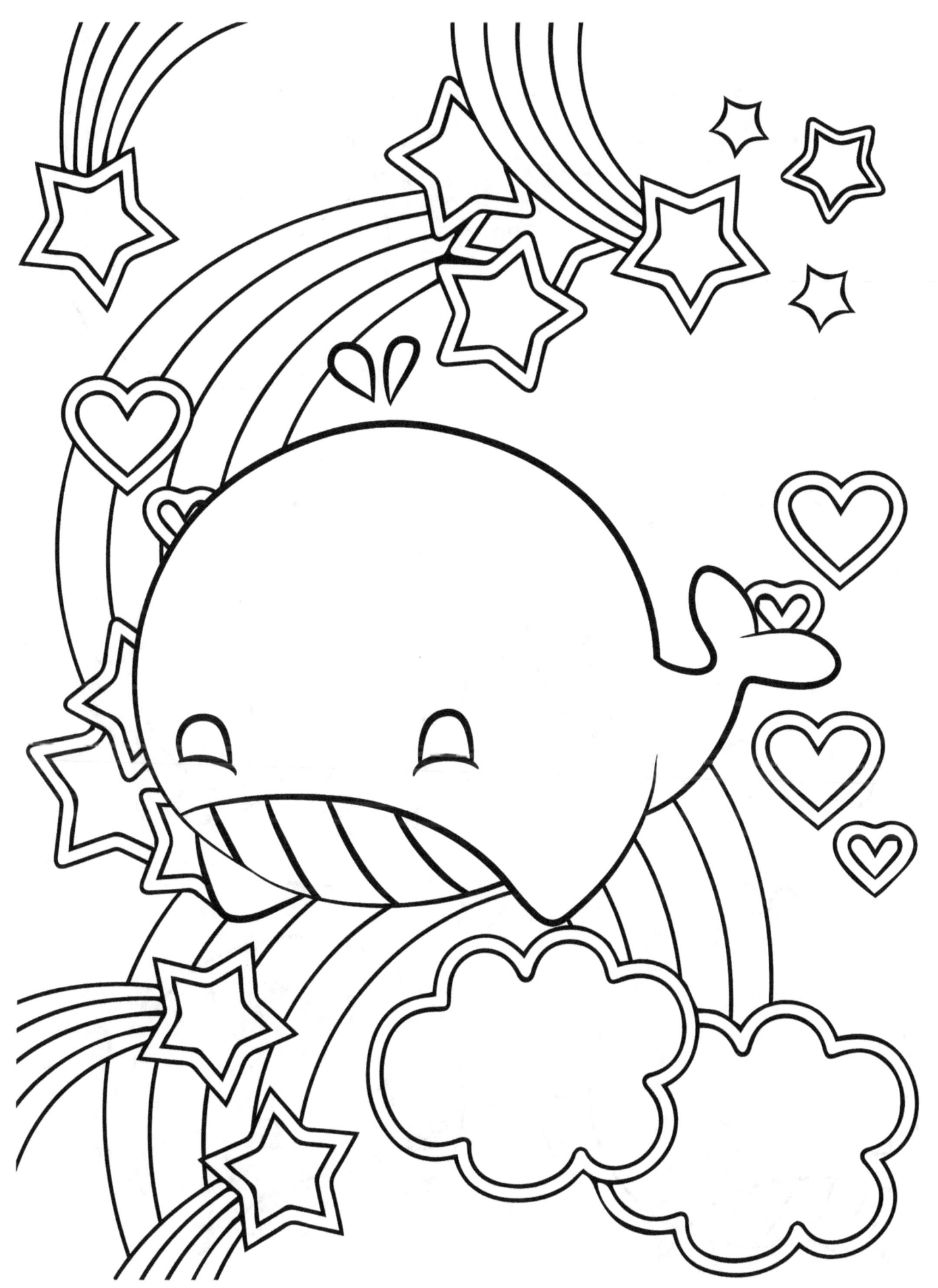

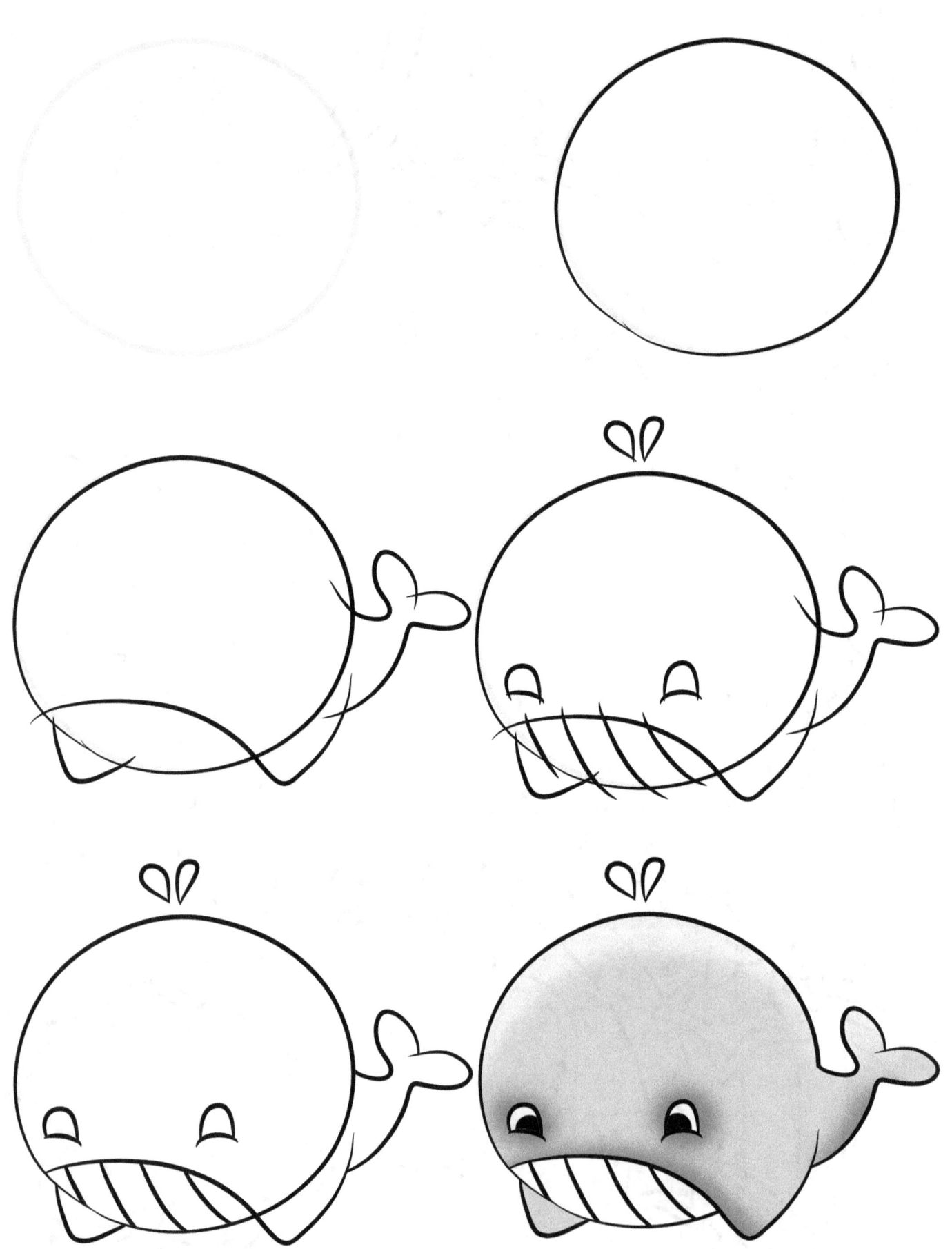

HOW TO DRAW CUTE ANIMALS FOR TODDLERS & KIDS

CUTE PETS FOR LEARN TO DRAW

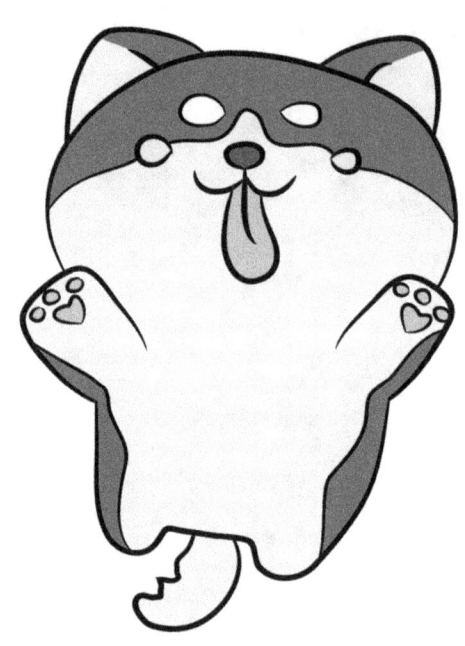

CUTE
FOR DRAWING
NEXT EDITION
COMONG SOON